AMILCAR CABRAL (1924–1973) was a Pan-African freedom fighter and anti-imperialist theorist. He was born in Bafatá, Guinea Bissau, under Portuguese colonial dominion. He studied agronomy in Portugal alongside other African colonial subjects who joined together to form student movements dedicated to opposing the ruling dictatorship of Portugal and to promoting the cause of independence for all Portuguese colonies in Africa. Upon his return to Africa in the 1950s, he managed, in under a decade, to lead Guinea Bissau toward near total independence before his assassination on January 20, 1973, by Portuguese agents.

TSENAY SEREQUEBERHAN is professor of philosophy at Morgan State University in Baltimore. He is the author of the groundbreaking work, *The Hermeneutics of African Philosophy: Horizon and Discourse,* and the key text, *African Philosophy: The Essential Readings*, among other books.

Return to the Source

Selected Texts of Amilcar Cabral

NEW EXPANDED EDITION

edited by TSENAY SEREQUEBERHAN

MONTHLY REVIEW PRESS
New York

Library of Congress Cataloging-in-Publication data
available from the publisher

ISBN paper: 978-1-68590-004-5
ISBN cloth: 978-1-68590-005-2

Typeset in Bulmer MT

MONTHLY REVIEW PRESS, NEW YORK
monthlyreview.org

5 4 3 2 1

Contents

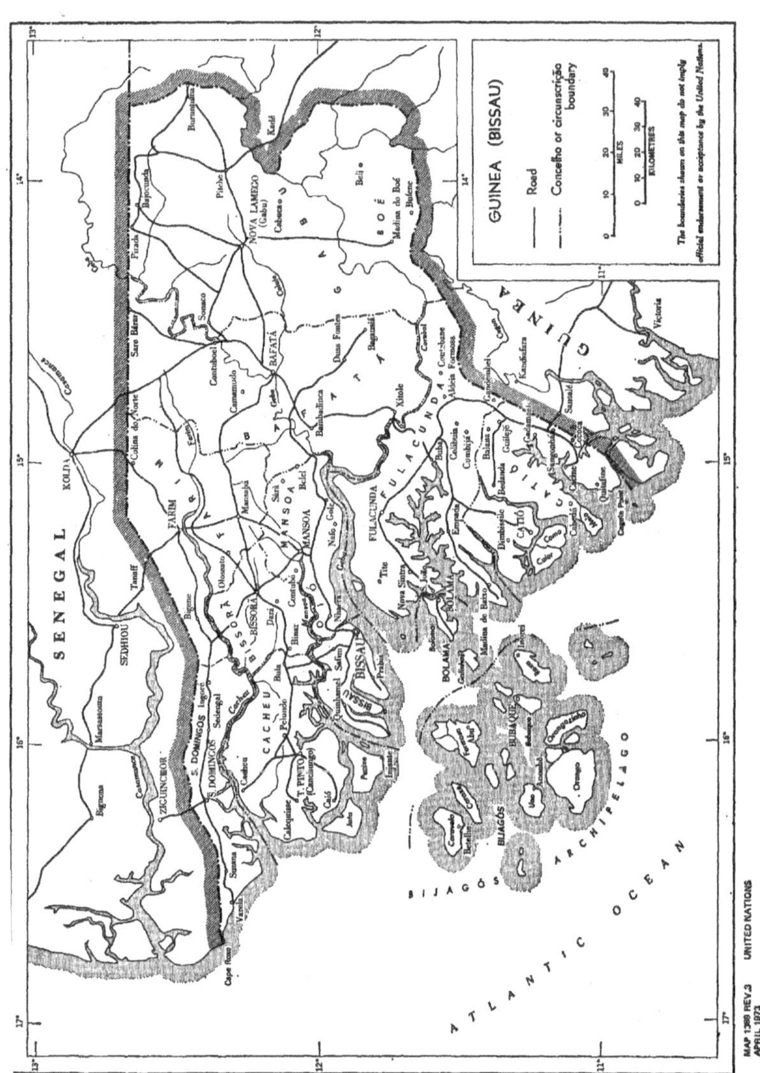

Guinea Bissau (Courtesy of the United Nations)

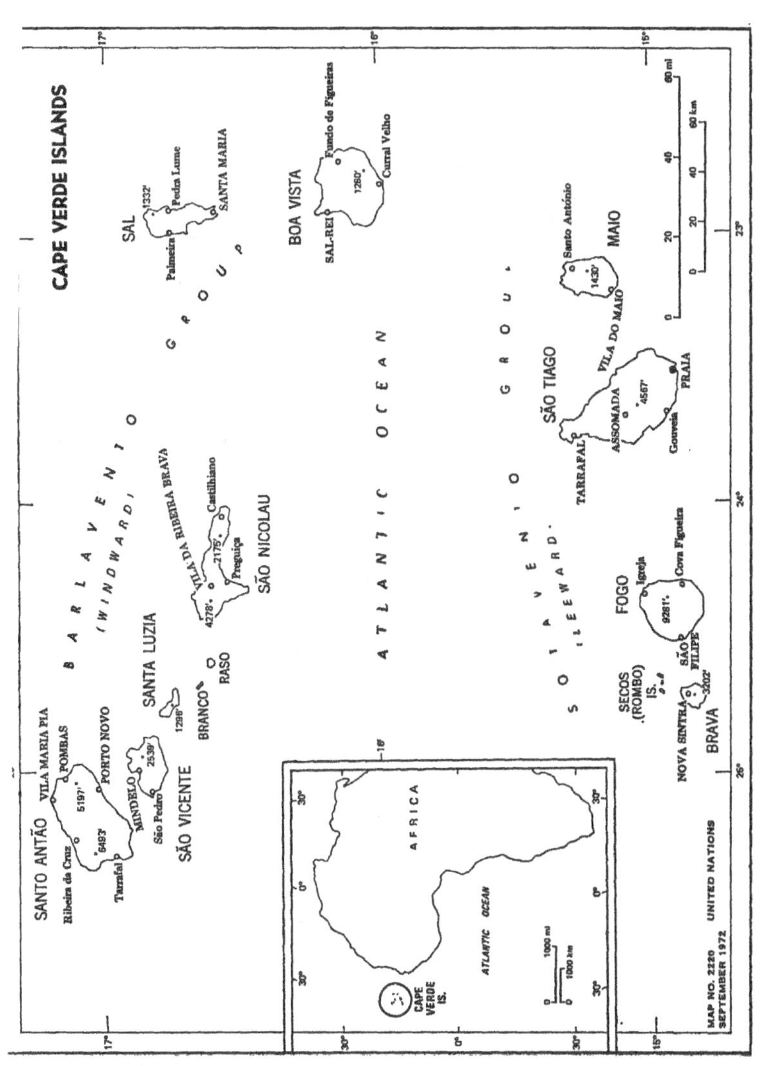

Cape Verde Islands (Courtesy of the United Nations)

Dedicated to the Struggle

Introduction to the Second Edition

Tsenay Serequeberhan

[I]ndependence has been turned into a cage, with people looking at us from outside the bars, sometimes with charitable compassion, sometimes with glee and delight.

—Patrice Lumumba

From Lumumba's last letter to his wife[1]

Amilcar Lopes da Costa Cabral was born of Cape Verdean parents in 1924 in Bafatá, the second largest city of Guinea-Bissau, in what was then "Portuguese" Guinea. He died, assassinated by Portuguese agents, in 1973, in the Republic of Guinea (Conakry).

After completing his high school education in Cape Verde in 1945, Cabral left for Portugal to attend the Technical University of Lisbon, from which he graduated in 1950 as an agronomist. In his student days in Lisbon, he participated with fellow students from the other two Portuguese colonies, Angola and Mozambique, in various engagements on differing levels of political militancy. This was a period when Cabral and his fellow students assessed the "mother" country and their stance toward it. It was a formative period in which assimilation was rejected and Africanness categorically affirmed.[2] Ideas initially considered and explored, during these formative years, were later consolidated and tailored to the specific actuality of the African anticolonial struggle.

Indeed, Cabral's importance lies in the specificity of his thought. His thinking is grounded in a principled fidelity to the historicity of the practice of struggle out of which it is articulated. His theorizing is a situated thinking; its originality arises out of its openness to the concrete possibilities of the situation at hand. At the time of his assassination at the age of 49, he had substantially explored, articulated, and concretely conceptualized—in this self-standing manner—crucial aspects of the African anticolonial struggle. He had formulated a conception of this struggle rooted in the historicity of the colonized. But what exactly does this mean in tangible terms?

In a 1970 interview with *Radio France Internationale*, in response to the question "Why Independence?" Cabral affirms the following:

> Yes, why independence? For us, from the outset, to be ourselves, to be African human beings, with all that which characterizes us, so as to advance towards a better life equipped and identified each day more with the peoples of the rest of the world. Salazar [António de Oliveira Salazar, dictator and Prime Minister of Portugal, 1932–1970] says that Africa does not exist without Europeans, this is an exaggeration the French are well placed to see. We consider that our independence will permit us to develop our own proper culture, to develop ourselves and to develop our country, deliver our people from misery, suffering, ignorance, because as you know this is the state in which we find ourselves after five centuries of Portuguese presence. We want independence not because we are racists, no, but because we are Africans, African human beings, an African people that today realizes its right to independence, to sovereignty . . . we want independence

> to make possible . . . a life in which we are not exploited by foreigners but also not by Africans . . . we do not see a link between skin color and exploitation.[3]

As should be clear from the above, for Cabral, the struggle against colonialism was not merely focused on ending foreign domination. Every mention, in the above remarks, to being "Africans, African human beings, an African people" presupposes, or has behind it, formulations of the anticolonial movement as a "return to the source" tailored to specific forms of struggle, conceived as a process of "re-Africanization."

These terms are not, for Cabral, empty slogans "bandied" about here and there for propaganda purposes. Nor are they the manifestation of a nostalgic yearning for the archaic African past. In each of them is encapsulated the position that the world we live in is specific to and inseparable from the ways in which we are involved with it. And this imposes on us the responsibility for our own existence. These theoretic constructs express Cabral's view of the anticolonial struggle, which he presents without cliché or predictable formulas. These are specific and creative conceptions that presuppose and address specified concerns.

Aimé Césaire, in *Discourse on Colonialism* (1955), had bluntly stated that "colonization = 'thingification.'"[4] A few years later, Frantz Fanon, in *The Wretched of the Earth* (1961), explored the ways in which "the colonized 'thing' becomes human in the very process through which it liberates itself."[5] Cabral, in his reflections on the anticolonial struggle, documented more amply in this second enlarged edition of *Return to the Source*, reflects on the specific process of struggle in and through which colonized Africa can overcome "thingification" and reclaim humanity. Cabral effectively explores the specifics through which this possibility can be properly appropriated.[6]

Now, in the context of the contemporary discourse of African philosophy, this is what the Cameroonian philosopher Marcien Towa refers to as the struggle to reclaim "our generic human identity."[7] This "generic human identity," mangled and markedly damaged by colonial subjugation, must be revitalized and tangibly reinstituted in constituting a truly independent and self-standing Africa. For Cabral, as for Towa, the termination of colonialism is not equal merely to the physical expulsion of the colonizer. It also, and more fundamentally, necessitates the purging/cleansing of the damage done to Africa's humanity, namely, the internalized servility and inferiority of the colonized.

In this respect, it can be said that Cabral expresses a perspective that—in effect and concretely—inaugurates and grounds the issues and concerns articulated by the militant segment of the contemporary discourse of African philosophy.[8] These are the concerns of the Africa that, in its victory over colonialism, has been vanquished by the residue of the past it had defeated. As Cabral puts it, "we want independence to make possible . . . a life in which we are not exploited by foreigners but also not by Africans." Today, Africa, as well as most of the formerly colonized world, is ruled by the suborn residue of the colonial past. Indeed:

> All post-colonial societies are still subject in one way or another to overt or subtle forms of neo-colonial domination, and independence has not solved this problem. The development of new elites within independent societies, often buttressed by neo-colonial institutions; the development of internal divisions based on racial, linguistic or religious discriminations; the continued unequal treatment of indigenous peoples in settler/invader societies—all these testify to the fact that post-colonialism is a continuing process of resistance and reconstruction.[9]

All the above, and Cabral's categoric affirmation that "we do not see a link between skin color and exploitation," makes clear that Cabral expresses a perspective that engages the specific issues and concerns of the dispossessed and subjugated majority of our postcolonial world. In Africa, he speaks for the Africa that, in victory, was disinherited by the dregs of the colonial past, that is, the African "replicant" ruling strata.[10]

Still, one could ask: What is the value of these texts today? The short answer to this question is that Cabral's work is timely and relevant! One need only flip through these pages to verify this assertion. In so doing, the reader will discover an insightful exploration of the complex issues and concerns that bedevil our postcolonial present.

Cabral engages in an inventory, *à la* Gramsci, of the "traces" of life—history and culture—that ground our present.[11] In the far-sighted manner of Fanon's "The Misadventures of National Consciousness," the third chapter of *The Wretched of the Earth*, Cabral explores the source of Africa's deplorable present condition. In this, he insists with Césaire on "the right to initiative."[12] On our right and responsibility to engage: "The singularity of our 'situation in the world' which is not to be confounded with any other."[13] And to have "the strength to invent instead of follow; the strength 'to invent' our way and rid it of ready-made forms, petrified forms which obstruct it."[14] Cabral tangibly models for us the theoretic and practical *way* of engaging the problems and concerns of our time. Insisting, in this, on veracity to the lived situation.

Those of us who have inherited the possibilities and limitations of the struggle for Africa's freedom need to reflect on and appropriate the *way* Cabral engages theoretic and practical concerns and issues. In so doing, we would become heirs to a tradition of thought generously endowed with an imaginative and critical disposition of mind. This would better position us to engage more aptly the specific and complex struggles that await us. Struggles focused on tangibly substantiating the formal and empty "freedom" of postcolonial Africa.

This is the calling of our present, just as those who came before us responded to the call for independence. Ours is a more complex struggle aimed at authenticating and consolidating, and thus validating, the "freedom" for which so many gave their lives.

As Fanon reminds us: "Each generation must out of a relative opacity discover its mission, fulfill it or betray it."[15] In keeping with this observation, to read Cabral is to explore a rich heritage of reflexive-reflective thought. It is to carry on the struggle to actualize the promise of a truly postcolonial Africa. To go beyond a *caged* "independence"—endorsed, sustained, and maintained by our former colonizers and the United States of America, the *patron saint* of our postcolonial neocolonial present.

Introduction to the First Edition

African Information Services

I am a simple African man, doing my duty in my own country in the context of our time.

—Amilcar Cabral (1924–1973)

The long and difficult struggle to free Africa from foreign domination has produced many heroic figures and will continue to produce many more. In some instances, individuals who seemed to be unlikely candidates emerged as spokesmen for the masses of their people. Often these were individuals who rejected avenues of escape from the realities of their people and who elected instead to return to the source of their own being. In taking this step, these individuals reaffirmed the right of their people to take their own place in history.

Amilcar Cabral is one such figure. And in the hearts of the people of the small West African country of Guinea (Bissau), he will remain a leader who helped them regain their identity and who was otherwise instrumental in the initial stages of the long and difficult process of national liberation.

Cabral is recognized as having been one of the world's outstanding political theoreticians. At the time of his assassination by Portuguese agents, on January 20, 1973—Cabral, as Secretary-General of the African Party for the Independence of Guinea and the Cape Verde Islands (PAIGC), was also an outstanding practitioner of these political theories. He had the ability to translate abstract theories into the concrete realities of his people, and very often the realities of his people resulted in the formulation of new theories.

The specific conditions of colonialism in Guinea (Bissau) and on the Cape Verde Islands were instrumental in the political development of Cabral. To his people, Portuguese colonialism meant a stagnant existence coupled with the absence of personal dignity and liberty. More than 99 percent of the population could not read or write. Sixty percent of the babies died before reaching the age of one year. Forty percent of the population suffered from sleeping sickness, and almost everyone had some form of malaria. There were never more than eleven doctors for the entire rural population, or one doctor for every 45,000 Africans.

In an effort to control the African population, Portugal attempted to create a minimally educated class, the members of which were granted the "privilege" of serving Portugal's interests. They were told to disdain everything African and to revere everything European. However, even if they adopted these attitudes, they were never really accepted by their masters.

The myth of Portugal's multi-racial society came to be exposed for what it was—a tool for little Portugal's continued domination of vast stretches of Africa.

Cabral studied in Portugal with Africans from other Portuguese colonies. This was a restive period in the development of African nationalist movements. The colonial powers had been weakened by the Second World War. And Africans had heard these powers speak of democracy, liberty, and human dignity—all of which were denied to the colonial subjects. Many Africans had even fought and died for the "liberty" of their colonial masters.

However, in the process, those who survived learned much about the world and themselves.

When Cabral was a student, his contemporaries included Agostinho Neto and Mario de Andrade (founding members of the Popular Movement for the Liberation of Angola-MPLA), and Eduardo Mondlane and Marcelino dos Santos (founding members of the Mozambique Liberation Front-FRELIMO). These men all rejected Portugal's right to define the lives of African people and committed themselves to struggle for change. As students, they strived to assert their national identities, and subsequently they returned to their respective countries to participate in the process of national liberation.

All of them saw that their people's enemy was not simply poverty, disease, or lack of education; nor was it the Portuguese people or simply whites; rather, it was colonialism and its parent imperialism. Cabral articulated this view in stating:

> We are not fighting against the Portuguese people, against individual Portuguese or Portuguese families. Without ever confusing the people of Portugal and Portuguese colonialism, we have been forced to take up arms in order to extirpate from the soil of our African fatherland, the shameful Portuguese colonial domination.[1]

This definition of the enemy proved an important ideological starting point. From here, revolutionary theories were formulated and put into practice, which resulted in the liberation of almost 75 percent of the countryside of Guinea (Bissau) in less than ten years of revolutionary armed struggle.

At the time of Cabral's murder, Guinea (Bissau) had virtually become an independent state with most of its principal towns occupied by a foreign army. In his Second Address at the United Nations, Cabral presented an overview of the struggle from its earliest days, and he described life in the liberated areas of his country. He described the process of national reconstruction in the face of continuous bombardments and attacks by Portuguese soldiers. And he announced the successful completion of freely held elections for a new National Assembly.

With each passing day, Portugal finds itself more and more isolated from the international community. Not even the death of Cabral can reverse the tide, which is running against one of the world's last remaining colonial rulers. In his New Year's Message, Cabral called on the PAIGC to press forward and continue the work necessary to issue a formal declaration of the new and independent state—Guinea (Bissau). This declaration will be issued during 1973 and will raise the struggle against Portuguese colonialism to another level.

The selections contained in this work illustrate a vital part of the study, analysis, and application which made it possible for the people of Guinea (Bissau), and their comrades in Mozambique and Angola, to achieve what they have achieved in the face of numerous difficulties. For example, in "Identity and Dignity in the Context of the National Liberation Struggle," Cabral discusses the "return to the source" as a political process rather than a cultural event.

He saw the process of returning to the source as being more difficult for those "native elites" who had lived in isolation from the "native masses" and developed feelings of frustration as a result of their ambiguous roles. Thus, he viewed movements which propounded strictly cultural or traditional views to be manifestations of the frustrations resulting from being isolated from the African reality.

Among the many truths left by Cabral is the fact that the process of returning to the source is of no historical importance (and would, in fact, be political opportunism) unless it involves not only a contest against the foreign culture but also complete participation in the mass struggle against foreign political and economic domination.

— 1 —

A Question-and-Answer Session
University of London, 27 October 1971

Comrades, I salute you all. It is a very great honor and a pleasure to have this opportunity of meeting you, not for a lecture, but for a friendly and, for us, a useful discussion. As I understand it, I am facing an audience of intellectuals—intellectuals in the good sense of the word. My responsibility is therefore great. I will do my best to answer the questions you put to me, and as briefly as possible, so as to have the maximum number of questions.

Question 1

What is the present military situation on the mainland of Guinea-Bissau? What are the military perspectives there and on the Cape Verde Islands?

You will be more or less aware of the military situation in my country. We have now liberated more than two-thirds of our national territory from the colonial yoke, and both our fight against the remaining Portuguese colonial positions, principally in the urban centers of the north, and also our political work in the Cape Verde Islands are intensifying day by day. Despite Portuguese bombings and other crimes, we have developed a new life in the liberated areas, where our people are increasingly the masters of their own destiny: this is fundamental to our armed struggle. However, in order to give you a fuller understanding of the current situation, I should like to go back to some of the essential factors that confronted us at the outset of our struggle.

Our country is unique in the African continent. We are in a flat part of Africa. The country divides basically into two regions: the coastal region and the interior. The coastal region, covered by rivers and swamps, extends as far as Mansoa, which is about 60 km from Bissau, and is characterized, from north to south, by forests and rice fields. The interior, from Mansoa to the eastern border, is lightly wooded savannah with occasional rivers. There are no mountains at all. Our people call the hills in Boé region, in the southeast, mountains, because in Guinea we don't really know what mountains are.

Another point is that our country is very small, only the size of Switzerland or Belgium. It is important to consider these geographical aspects of Guinea in relation to the liberation struggle because, as you know, the manuals of guerrilla warfare generally state that a country has to be of a certain size to be able to create what is called a base, and, further, that mountains are the best place to develop guerrilla warfare. Obviously, we don't have those conditions in Guinea, but this did not stop us beginning our armed liberation struggle.

I would like to make it clear that we took up this struggle only in answer to the violent oppression of our people by the Portuguese colonialists. We are not fighting because we are a warlike people, or because we think armed struggle is the only means. In some circumstances, however, it may be the only means, and even the best means. It all depends on the particular conditions of the country involved. What we did was to establish a strategy based on the principle: "Start from the actual conditions of Guinea," the geographical, social, historical, political, and economic conditions.

Basing ourselves on this principle, we studied our social

structure as deeply as we could, together with all other factors likely to influence the eventual development of our struggle. As for the mountains, we decided that our people had to take their place, since it would be impossible to develop our struggle otherwise. So our people are our mountains. To achieve this, we adopted another principle—self-evident, it seemed to us—that our struggle is a political one, which takes an armed form because of the Portuguese colonialists, but it is from beginning to end a political struggle. We are not fighting to invade Portugal, or to enter Lisbon. We are fighting for the independence of our own country.

On this basis we prepared the political ground necessary for the armed struggle to develop. The first step was to mobilize and organize our people politically; this took about three years. For this we adopted another principle, based on a national proverb which says, "Rice can only be cooked inside a pot." Even if you have fire, you can't cook rice outside the pot. This means that our struggle has to be carried on inside our own country; from the beginning we had to avoid any diversion of our efforts through the use of neighboring countries. This is very important, because the general tendency is to take advantage of the facilities you have abroad to fight from the outside inwards.

Owing to our small population, we adopted a further principle: To fight as economically as possible, since we can afford only the minimum of losses. So we worked out our strategy and tactics. And I can say that I know of no other liberation struggle where losses have been fewer than ours.

We also agreed that our strategy had to be centrifugal. As you know, the Portuguese believed that we would develop our forces outside, in neighboring countries, and then move in towards the center of Guinea. They therefore concentrated their troops on the borders. But we began the general armed struggle in 1963 from the interior of Guinea, at a place south of the Geba River. That is to say, we did the exact opposite of what the Portuguese expected—we moved from the center outwards.

Furthermore, from the start of the struggle, we did our utmost to give the maximum autonomy to our guerrilla units. This was risky but necessary, as it was not initially possible for us, even in a small country like ours, to have day-to-day direction of every guerrilla unit. Yet it was a decision that contained some dangers for our struggle.

Clearly, there are some basic contradictions in a struggle like ours. The main contradiction, our great difficulty, is that we have to fight against a foreign power in our own land. They destroy our people and our resources, but we cannot go to Lisbon, or to the villages of Portugal, to retaliate. This makes our struggle a hard one. If it had been possible, at the beginning, for us to attack the enemy in their own country, less fighting would have been necessary. But the Portuguese have a very powerful advantage. They bring their men and their arms to fight against us, destroying our villages, and they also oblige us to destroy our own property. Yet we can never touch them in their own country. So, as part of our strategy, we have had to develop tactics that enable us, as far as possible, to avoid the destruction of our own country.

On the colonialists' side, too, there is a comparable contradiction: In order to dominate Guinea they have to be there, occupying it. For Guinea is not Portugal; it is an African country only conquered in the first place after fifty years of colonial war. And, in order to maintain the conquest, they have to be present. At first, the presence was military; later, when they had established an administration, they used civil control, with all the apparatus of a colonial state. When we launched our armed struggle, the Portuguese were compelled to reinforce their presence—they brought in troops and distributed them all over the country, in the villages as well as the urban centers, to maintain their domination.

But this dispersion of the enemy forces meant weakness, and our strategy was to concentrate specific forces to attack the Portuguese place by place. They suffered losses immediately, and made the fatal move of concentrating their forces in order to defend themselves. But this meant leaving large parts of the country outside their control. This was, and is, a dilemma that cannot be solved in a colonial war: when they disperse their forces so as to maintain control, we concentrate ours so as to attack them, thus forcing them to concentrate. But when their forces are concentrated, we organize, mobilize, and develop new structures in the countryside, so that they can never come back.

What are the main strategic objectives of the colonial army? Firstly, to maintain their positions in the urban centers. Secondly, to disperse their forces to assure domination.

To supply their troops they must control the main arteries of communication. In Guinea this means principally the roads but also the rivers, because a lot of communication is by river. This the Portuguese did. At first, they had more than eighty garrisons, large and small, distributed all over our country; they controlled the main roads and were able to travel freely along all navigable rivers. I recall that boats of ten thousand tons used to go up the Farim River as far as the internal port of Tambato, where Guinea groundnuts are loaded for export.

To destroy this system of domination, we simply concentrated our forces and attacked two camps simultaneously—Tite and Fulacunda. Most of the Portuguese troops were at the time in the border areas and in Bissau. They started to move immediately, heading for the center of the country. But our guerrillas were all over the roads, cutting trees to make roadblocks, laying mines and ambushes. We caused heavy losses; six months later, the Portuguese Minister of Defense, General Araujo, had to make a press statement admitting that we were in control of 15 percent of the territory. It was the best propaganda we could have had, especially as our struggle was up till then unknown outside Guinea. We concentrated our forces for attack, we dispersed them to ambush the main roads, and we started trying to close off the rivers.

Since that point, we have made great progress. Altogether, we have expelled the Portuguese from more than forty camps—from some small camps in both the north and the south, and more recently from important ones such as Madina and Beli. For an example, the Portuguese used to have fourteen camps along the border with Guinea [Conakry]. Now they have only one, in the east.

We now control all the main roads except some in the western and central-eastern regions. The Portuguese cannot use them and don't even try. Recently, they made efforts to asphalt the roads so they could use them, but it's really too late for them to asphalt roads because we have become very efficient at destroying their transport with bazookas and other weapons. On the roads still occasionally used by Portuguese troops, we destroyed ninety trucks and armored cars between January and August 1971; on the rivers we sank twenty Portuguese boats during the same period, having over the years developed our capacity to attack river craft.

At the moment, the Portuguese have about thirty-five garrisons, including Bissau, Bafata, and the other main towns. But almost all the roads in the hinterland are closed to them. And we are increasing our assaults on the urban centers still under occupation by the colonialists; last June we launched our first attacks on Portuguese positions in Bissau and Bafata. In all the rural areas, we are free and sovereign—that is more than two-thirds of the country.

That summarizes the general military situation in Guinea at present. As far as the perspective of the struggle is concerned (the second part of the question) the aim is to fight until victory. We are determined to fight, not only with arms, but also through political work and national reconstruction in the liberated regions. We are determined to increase our attacks on Portuguese positions. We are also determined to develop and intensify our political activity in the Cape Verde Islands. All depends, naturally, on technical problems, but the party is now in a position politically to change the nature of the struggle in the Cape Verde Islands.

Question 2

Why has Portugal been notoriously unable to seek some kind of neocolonial solution? Have Portuguese tactics changed in any measure in response to the armed struggle?

This is an important point. Many people ask how it is possible for Portugal, the most underdeveloped and backward country in Europe—not the fault of the Portuguese people, but the fault of her ruling classes—to continue to wage three colonial wars in Africa, as they have done for over ten years now, since the start of the war in Angola. How and why? The first answer is that it is precisely because Portugal is underdeveloped, that she is unable to find a solution for her colonies, because she cannot hope for a neocolonialist one.

In analyzing the problems of African independence, we can say that independence was given to colonized countries by the colonial powers as a means of securing the indirect domination of colonized peoples. But Portugal does not possess the necessary economic infrastructure that will allow her to try decolonization in this manner. She cannot decolonize because she cannot neocolonize.

Clearly, the Portuguese economy is not strong enough to support colonial wars. But it is very difficult for the ruling class in Portugal to adapt to reality because they themselves are trapped within the psychology of underdevelopment, from which have sprung all their "theories" of multi-racialism, non-racialism, multi-continentalism, Luso-tropicalism, etc. All Portuguese culture is impregnated with this type of thinking, and it stems from the economic conditions and the form of class domination that prevail in Portugal. Portugal's own condition means that she cannot seek a solution of the neocolonial variety, because Portugal herself is a semi-colony. Even the telephones in Portugal are not of Portuguese manufacture, nor the tramways, nor the railways. The mines of São Domingos and São Justo are not wholly Portuguese-owned. The Portuguese in this room know all this very well, better than I. So there can be no question of a neocolonial solution.

Has Portugal changed her tactics in response to our armed struggle? We were very innocent when we began. We thought it was possible to persuade Portugal to change, possible to use peaceful means to make her change. But the Portuguese colonialists soon taught us that it wasn't possible to fight them empty-handed, that we had to try and force them to change. It was only when we Africans realized that peaceful means were useless that we launched our armed struggle—first in Angola, later in Guinea, and finally in Mozambique. And now the Portuguese colonialists are changing, they are changing.

Their tactics have changed already. Salazar, in fact, was a very limited man, a man with a feudal mentality, and he was independent. He served the ruling classes, but from a position of independence, and by force of his strong personality. Caetano is none of these things. Salazar was a great figure only at Coimbra University. But Caetano taught at the Lisbon Faculty of Law and was also a member of the Council of Bank Administration—a true servant of Portuguese capitalism, completely dependent on the ruling class.

Yet Caetano had thus a wider experience than Salazar, and he began in the political field a kind of so-called change. In Guinea he tried a new policy, making concessions to the urban people while still controlling them. You know how it's done—build a new school or two, enroll more people in schools, send them on free trips to Mecca and Fatima, give them the titles "madame" and "monsieur." Before they were merely things, now they're called names like "splendissima senhora" [splendid lady]. And the Portuguese believe we will be fooled by these gestures. But they're failing miserably in this.

Of course, the colonialists try to divide our people. On one hand, they tell us that Portugal is one multi-racial, multi-continental nation—we are all one family and so on. And changes were made in the Portuguese Constitution in 1951, after the adoption of the UN Charter, with further changes following in 1961 after the UN resolution on decolonization. Indeed, during the history of Portugal, the colonies have changed names many times. During the first Republic, they were called colonies, but later they became "overseas provinces," to avoid any defense of their rights to self-determination by the democratic and progressive forces of the world. After colonies, after overseas provinces, what new name will they find?

On the other hand, after the beginning of our struggle in 1960, other kinds of changes were introduced into the Constitution for all three colonies. For example, two sorts of people had been identified in Guinea—the "natives" and the "assimilados." The natives form 99.7 percent of the population. The assimilados—after 500 years—are a mere 0.3 percent.

Portugal claims to encourage assimilation but in fact obstructs it, because her rulers know quite well that if people become assimilated, they can't be so easily exploited. (Not that we want to be assimilated. On the contrary, we want to be ourselves. But it was better to be assimilated than native, because a native can be subjected to forced labor, and has to pay a poll tax on himself, his wife, and his children. There are taxes for second and third wives, too—very neat, that.)

There are now further changes in the Constitution. The new idea is called "progressive autonomy" for our country. However, if you study Caetano's recent law to this effect, and his speeches on it, you will see that it means nothing, absolutely nothing. The Portuguese are fooling themselves—they've told so many lies that they're beginning to believe these lies themselves.

The main political change that has occurred in Guinea is the fact that General Spínola, military governor of Bissau, is now claiming, not only that he will lead our people forward to self-determination under the Portuguese flag, but also that he will create a social revolution in the country. That's very strange, because in Portugal it's illegal to talk about "social revolution." You can't even use the word "social"; it's considered a dangerous word. And "revolution"—much more terrible! Now, it would be very nice for us if Portugal had a social revolution. That would mean our independence would be granted willingly and we shouldn't have to fight for it. So we suggest General Spínola goes back to his own country and creates a social revolution there. He could also develop the Portuguese economy while he's at it—it's one of the most backward in Europe.

Question 3

How will you move from the structure of a guerrilla struggle to structures for mass participation in a new state? How will you reduce the danger of the leadership becoming detached from the people?

In Guinea, guerrilla struggle means mass participation. Without mass participation the guerrilla struggle would be impossible. Perhaps in other conditions it may be possible, but in Guinea the only way is through mass participation.

The problem that this question refers to is the practical application of some of the theoretical ideas about guerrilla struggle. Our movement can only be said to have had a guerrilla struggle structure during the first year of fighting—if that, because it wasn't a guerrilla-struggle structure in the sense of a structure that led the people. We began with our political organization: We are, and have always been, first of all a party—a national liberation movement constituted by a party that leads the people to liberation. Our guerrilla forces, even when they were fewer and more autonomous, were specifically created as the military arm of the party. In Guinea there is no question of the guerrillas directing the party: the guerrilla is at all times under the direction of the party.

This is important. Since our Congress of Cassaca in 1964, we have maintained a clear distinction between the functions of the different instruments of the party. We distinguished between the role of the party, whose main task lies in political work, and the role of the armed forces, guerrilla or regular, whose task is to take action against the Portuguese colonialists. At the same time, we created all the organs necessary for national reconstruction work in liberated areas.

We have therefore no really great problems in moving from the structure of a guerrilla struggle to the structures of mass participation. We are organized as a party: by village, by zone, and by region. Southern Guinea is led by the National Committee of Liberated Regions in the South, and the north is led by the National Committee of Liberated Regions in the North. This forms a basic structure of government. The liberated regions in fact already contain all the elements of a state—administrative services, health services, education services, local armed forces for defense against Portuguese attacks, tribunals, and prisons. The immediate problem is to move from the liberated to the non-liberated areas, and to enlarge our state till it encloses the whole country. The transition to state structure will not be a problem.

The second part of the question asked how the danger of the leadership becoming detached from the people can be reduced. This is a constant problem, a constant struggle. But we have based our struggle on our masses, and their participation in the decisions taken for the movement by the party is continually increasing. In the liberated regions we are now preparing for the election of local assemblies, and the election of our first national assembly. We believe this will reinforce the sovereignty of our people and enlarge the democratic basis of our actions now and in the future. Up till now, all decisions concerning our struggle have been taken by the organs of the party, but after the elections of the assemblies, matters affecting each region will be studied and decided by regional assemblies. Naturally, military problems are a separate matter: the council of war decides those. We believe that the fact that the people are represented in the committees of the party, in the popular tribunals, and will be represented, after the elections, in the assemblies, means that it should be possible to prevent the leadership becoming detached from the led.

But we shall have to be vigilant. For this reason: the idea of the struggle against the enemy was launched by elements of the petite bourgeoisie—by the revolutionary petite bourgeoisie if you like—with the peasants and urban workers joining in later to provide the essential basis for the struggle. But the normal tendency of the petite bourgeoisie is towards bourgeois behavior—to want to be the boss—and development of the struggle can crystallize in this way. Indeed, this happens not only with petit bourgeois elements, but also with the peasant people; there is always a strong tendency for the framework of the movement to acquire a bourgeois caste. We must be very wary of this today, and more especially in the future.

Can the danger be reduced? We can reduce it only by constantly reinforcing the participation and control by the mass over the whole liberation movement. When we began, there were just six of us in Bissau—two workers and four petit bourgeois. Later, as the workers in the urban centers joined, the group was partly transformed. And today, the majority of the party leadership comes from the peasant element, and the majority of our comrades in the struggle are peasants, and in all our liberated regions the peasants are armed. At the beginning [of the struggle], our man [that is, a militant of the movement] was a very great man when he entered the village with a gun; with a weapon he was a privileged person. Now a weapon means nothing; all the villagers have them. But we have not yet achieved absolute equality in the movement; it remains an important question for the future.

Question 4

In the building of a new society in Guinea-Bissau, what will be the guiding lines of economic organization?

I'll be brief on this. We consider that the guiding lines in economic affairs are simply that there shall be no more exploitation of our people. We have had enough exploitation. We have been exploited by the traditional chiefs, by other sections of our society, and by the colonial power. That's quite enough.

Nor do we see any difference between one form of exploitation and another, when all that changes is the color of the exploiters' skin. So, no more exploitation either by foreigners or by our own people. To achieve this, however, we will have to be realistic and pay extremely close attention to our actual situation.

We are an agricultural country—but a backward agricultural country. The Portuguese never developed Guinea agriculturally; tractors and fertilizers are largely unknown. Our first objective at this stage is to ensure that agriculture remains the most important focus of our economic policy, and this means that our principal task will have to be a technical revolution in agriculture.

Naturally, people in Europe expect "agrarian reform" in my country. But in Guinea (Cape Verde is a different matter) the problem of agrarian reform is not the same as it is in Europe. This is because the land is not privately owned in Guinea. The Portuguese did not occupy our land as settlers, as, for example they did in Angola. The African kept the land and the Portuguese appropriated the fruits of his labor. As a result, most of the land has remained the property of the villages. Of course, in tribes like the Fula or Mandjak, which have a pyramidal social structure, the chiefs have the best land. But they have it only in terms of getting the best possible production from it; they do not own it, for it cannot be sold or otherwise disposed of.

We do not therefore have the problem of agrarian reform in relation to land ownership that other countries are familiar with. What we need is an agrarian revolution to improve the yield of the soil through technology, and we believe that the best structure for this change will be a cooperative system. There is, in fact, a tradition of cooperation in our country between members of the same family, between different families and even between different villages. Some Africans have called this a cooperative system, arguing that the African family constitutes a ready-made cooperative. This is not really so; a true cooperative does not exist when some members still exploit others—in Fula society, for instance, where the women work but have no rights—that's in no sense a true cooperative.

We believe that we must develop the cooperative as the fundamental economic structure in our way of life, not only internally as the basis of our whole economy, but also in terms of our country's international economic relations. We believe we should try to act as a nation in the same way as a cooperative acts, within a system of international cooperatives. I cannot now go into all the details of our thinking on this matter, but I have explained the basic guidelines of our economic organization.

Question 5

How do you see the relationship between the armed struggle in the three Portuguese territories and the condition of the rest of the African continent?

The three-armed struggles in Mozambique, Angola, and Guinea are closely linked, for several reasons. Firstly, we are fighting the same enemy—Portuguese colonialism. Secondly, but no less importantly, the leaders of the three movements began by working together; we were people of the Portuguese colonies before we were Guinean, Mozambican, or Angolan, and we worked together in Lisbon, sharing in the creation of the three movements.

Political reasons also keep us together. At the outset, our struggle in Guinea for instance, provoked a feeling of insecurity among the neighboring states, but as the struggle grew and strengthened in Africa, it became a positive force. Our struggles in Angola, Mozambique, and Guinea now aid the security of surrounding countries who are also menaced by the Portuguese colonialists. This is the first effect of our liberation movements as far as the rest of Africa is concerned.

The second effect is that we are showing Africans it is possible to transform one's life; it is possible to fight the great colonialist-imperialist powers in our continent. Our struggle is part of the making of African history.

We also believe that our struggle helps to influence the attitudes of people in other dominated African countries, especially in Southern Africa, although, of course, we are also aware that whatever other peoples can do by way of destroying colonialism or racism in their countries helps our struggle enormously. We could talk about this for hours; that's the briefest answer I can give you.

Question 6

You have been quoted as being willing to reach a negotiated settlement with the Portuguese. Would this allow an outlet "with honor" for the Portuguese, which would not damage their morale and would therefore allow them to intensify their actions in Angola and Mozambique?

Our position on the question of negotiation is very clear: our battle is emphatically a political battle. We are not fighting to conquer Portugal; we are fighting to liberate our country from the colonial yoke. I can perhaps illustrate this by relating the story of the Italian journalist who interviewed a schoolboy in the north of Guinea, asking: "Aren't you tired of this long struggle?" The child replied: "It's for the Portuguese to tire of it; we shan't tire because it's our country." Journalist: "But how will it end?" The child: "Well, in the beginning it was only politics, and in the end, it will be only politics too." A fourteen-year-old child.

Anyone with revolutionary ideas who doesn't understand that our struggle has to include negotiations doesn't understand anything. We are always ready for negotiations. Our fundamental principle is this: We are fighting to gain the independence of our country, and to redeem all the sacrifices we have agreed upon during these long years of struggle. Independence is the only solution.

It may be true that if independence is won in Guinea and the

Cape Verdes through negotiation, the Portuguese will be enabled to intensify their war against Angola and Mozambique. But if the fatalism of this hypothetical argument is accepted, we will none of us have independence—not Angola nor Mozambique nor my country. Because if Angola wins her independence first, seventy thousand troops will come into little Guinea and occupy all the villages, and the same if Mozambique is freed. No, it's a false problem. The Portuguese know very well if they are thrown out of one of the three countries, it will be the end for them in the other two as well. Public opinion in Portugal will demand the wholesale liberation of the African territories, and even the Portuguese troops will refuse to fight.

You may recall that France, trying to prevent the liberation of Algeria, gave independence to the other colonies, to avoid having to fight there as well. It might be independence in name only, but the very fact that it was given strengthened the fight in Algeria. The struggle for independence is a process that cannot be reversed.

Question 7

You have also been quoted as being willing to discuss independence for mainland Guinea without the Cape Verde Islands. How do you defend this statement against the charge that it is potentially a betrayal of one-fifth of your constituency?

The press is in fact slightly mistaken about our position on the Cape Verde Islands. At my press conference I was asked, "What will your position be if the Portuguese decide to grant independence to Guinea without the Cape Verde Islands?" My reply was, "We are ready to negotiate and we will answer this question if and when the Portuguese ask it, not when you do." The Portuguese, you see, have launched some trial balloons in order to ascertain our position in advance, but obviously we can't answer, except directly to them during negotiating. However, we are ready to discuss the issue, as we said. This doesn't mean we shall concede it; we are the African Party for the Independence of Guinea and the Cape Verdes. But we know that there can be more than one way of achieving the same aim, just as we know that even twins are not born at exactly the same moment. What we can assure the comrade who put this question is that we shall not cease our struggle before the total independence of Guinea and the Cape Verde Islands. We are one country, one people.

Question 8

You have said you would be prepared to talk to the Portuguese. What is your position vis-à-vis "dialogue" with the racist regime in South Africa?

The problem is what kind of dialogue and with whom? We consider it to be a real betrayal for the head of an African state to want a dialogue with the racists of South Africa, disregarding the rights of the people of that country. And don't muddle Banda [former dictator of Malawi] up with the idea of dialogue. Banda isn't having a "dialogue," he is the servant of the South African racists. We are in favor of any kind of initiative from the independent African states that will facilitate negotiations between the South African racist regime and the nationalists in South Africa. But we do not recognize the right of any head of state in Africa to negotiate with the racist regime in the nationalists' place. Our position on this is quite clear and we could not adopt any other.

But I hope this problem of negotiation is fully understood. The aim of the struggle is negotiation. We do not criticize the Vietnamese people for negotiating a peace treaty with the American imperialists; to do that would show one understood nothing of the struggle.

Question 9

What light has your experience of the armed struggle thrown upon theories of armed struggle current in the last decade?

We think that our experience is *our* experience. It's very difficult to say how our experience can help others, although we are sure it can be useful for others to study it so as to understand the priorities in their own countries, not necessarily by adopting other people's policies.

There are, of course, general laws of the theory of armed struggle for national liberation. These laws cover, for instance, those contradictions I mentioned earlier. Firstly, that we cannot counterattack the enemy on his home ground (up till now, anyway; perhaps the anti-imperialists will give us planes and warships so we can go to Portugal and finish this whole business off). Secondly, the contradiction that the colonial forces have to disperse themselves to assure domination, but in doing so, become vulnerable.

But every theory of armed struggle has to arise as the consequence of an actual armed struggle. In every case, practice comes first, theory later. Yet it's wrong to suppose that it can be entirely empirical, for each struggle contains something shared by all other struggles and something that it creates for itself on the basis of the general experience—just as with art, if you like. Picasso is a very great and original artist, but he is also the product of other artists who preceded him. It's the same with the armed struggle. If you really want to advance the struggle, you must make a critical assessment of the experience of others before applying their theories, but the basic theory of armed struggle has to come from the reality of the fight.

Let me put it like this: it's possible for a scientist, working away in a closed room, to think about all the relations between the planets and stars, taking into account all the forces and movements and cosmic dynamics, and to speculate that another planet exists. For the liberation movement, these armchair methods are impossible. No one could create the theory of the struggle for liberation without participating in the struggle. There are, of course, some people—and very brave they are, too—who write manuals of guerrilla warfare without having taken part in a guerrilla war, but that's not our fault. All the true manuals of guerrilla war have been written by people who have taken part.

So, to summarize my answer to this question: if you have to wage a guerrilla war, please study the real, the concrete conditions that face you. Be familiar with the experience of others, but try to find your own solution, your own method of fighting.

Question 10

Besides nationalism, is your struggle founded on any ideological basis? To what extent has the ideology of Marxism and Leninism been relevant to the prosecution of the war in Guinea-Bissau? What practical peculiarities, if any, have necessitated the modification of Marxism-Leninism?

We believe that a struggle like ours is impossible without ideology. But what kind of ideology? I will perhaps disappoint many people here when I say that we do not think ideology is a religion. A religion tells one, for example, that Christ was born in Nazareth and performed this miracle and that and so on and so on, and one believes it or one doesn't believe it, and one practices the religion or one doesn't. Moving from the realities of one's own country towards the creation of an ideology for one's struggle doesn't imply that one has pretensions to be a Marx or a Lenin or any other great ideologist, but is simply a necessary part of the struggle. I confess that we didn't know these great theorists terribly well when we began. We didn't know them half as well as we do now! We needed to know them, as I've said, in order to judge in what measure we could borrow from their experience to help our situation—but not necessarily to apply the ideology blindly just because it's a very good ideology. That is where we stand on this.

But ideology is important in Guinea. As I've said, never again do we want our people to be exploited. Our desire to develop our country with social justice and power in the hands of the people is our ideological basis. Never again do we want to see a group or a class of people exploiting or dominating the work of our people. That's our basis. If you want to call it Marxism, you may call it Marxism. That's your responsibility. A journalist once asked me, "Mr. Cabral, are you a Marxist?" Is Marxism a religion? I am a freedom fighter in my country. You must judge from what I do in practice. If you decide that it's Marxism, tell everyone that it is Marxism. If you decide it's not Marxism, tell them it's not Marxism. But the labels are your affair; we don't like those kinds of labels. People here are very preoccupied with the questions: Are you Marxist or not Marxist? Are you Marxist-Leninist? Just ask me, please, whether we are doing well in the field. Are we really liberating our people, the human beings in our country, from all forms of oppression? Ask me simply this and draw your own conclusions.

We cannot, from our experience, claim that Marxism-Leninism must be modified—that would be presumptuous. What we must do is to modify, to radically transform, the political, economic, social, and cultural conditions of our people. This doesn't mean that we have no respect for all that Marxism and Leninism have contributed to the transformation of struggles throughout the world and over the years. But we are absolutely sure that we have to create and develop in our particular situation the solution for our country. We believe that the laws governing the evolution of all human societies are the same. Our society is developing in the same way as other societies in the world, according to the historical process; but we must understand clearly what stage our society has reached. Marx, when he created Marxism, was not a member of a tribal society; I think there's no necessity for us to be more Marxist than Marx or more Leninist than Lenin in the application of their theories.

Question 11

Can you comment on the realities of classes in Africa? How suitable are the correct ideological weapons of class analysis for African liberation movements, social revolution, and unity?

First of all, the question about the realities of class in Africa is too wide a question. Although we are in favor of unity from the Mediterranean to the Cape, we must recognize that there is not "one Africa." Historically, economically, culturally, Africa is not one. The class situation in one country is very different from that in another. Moreover, it is not for me, at this stage of the struggle, to analyze the realities of classes in other countries.

As far as Guinea is concerned, our analysis of the class and social structure of our country has been made; it is published in *Revolution in Guinea*, the book produced by our friend Richard Handyside.[1] I'm not just making propaganda for his talents as editor: you'll appreciate there isn't time for me to make a full class analysis of Guinea now, especially when it is already available. I would simply like to remind those who put the question about ideology that when we began to mobilize our people, we couldn't mobilize them for the struggle against imperialism—nor even, in some areas of Guinea, for the struggle against colonialism—because the people didn't know what the words meant. You have no difficulty in understanding what imperialism and colonialism are, but we who were suffering the effects of colonialist-imperialist domination didn't know what it meant.

So we had to mobilize our people on the basis of the daily realities of suffering and exploitation, and now, even the children in Guinea know what colonialism and imperialism are. Again, we couldn't mobilize the people of Guinea under the slogan of "land for those who work the land," because our people take for granted the fact that everyone will have land since there is no shortage of land. As a slogan it may have strong ideological content, but it doesn't happen to be relevant to Guinea. It is essential to link ideological weapons to the reality of the situation. It is right that those who fight should forge a correct ideological weapon for their country. But it is very difficult, I repeat, to define a general correct ideological weapon for all African countries.

Question 12

What are the class differences between the town people and the country people in Guinea, and what effect do these differences have on a) the organization of the party and b) the methods of liberation?

Again, the full answer to this can be found in *Revolution in Guinea* [The relevant texts, referred to by Cabral, are included in the present volume as chapters 3 and 5.] I would, however, like to make just this point: that towns in Guinea are not like your towns, with centuries of existence as crystallized cities, behind them. A majority of our townspeople are first-generation—half peasant—and a large proportion of them still have their parcel of land in the rural areas, to which they return to work periodically, alternating between town and country. There are thus more links between town and country in Guinea than in Europe or indeed in many other African countries.

So there is no great contradiction between the urban worker and the rural worker, as far as the African laborer class is concerned. However, within the urban population there are several different groups, or layers. There is the colonial class, which mainly refers to the Portuguese administration but also includes certain Africans; there is the petite bourgeoisie; there are the white-collar workers in the state administration and in commercial business; there are the workers, who are not a working class as exists in Britain, but who are wage earners; and finally there are those who live from hand to mouth.

In the countryside, there is no homogeneous rural society in Guinea, as *Revolution in Guinea* explains. Classifications cannot be made on a national basis, as everything is complicated by the fact that there are several different ethnic groups, ranging from the Balante to the Fula, with wide differences of social structure. Between these two extreme types there are many variations of social organization.

That is a summary of the differences between town and

country people in Guinea, but I would like to emphasize that, even in the towns, the people are influenced by these rural or tribal structures: a Balante is a Balante even in the town, and a Fula the same. Though it remains true that the creation of towns has radically transformed our country, as, for example did the introduction of money.

What effect does this social analysis have on the decisions of our party, once we have studied all the links between the structures? Well, I could talk about this subject for hours—the links between, and the effects of, the social structure on the organization of struggle and of methods of liberation. But I will have to refer you again to *Revolution in Guinea*.

At this point, though there were many more questions and an enthusiastic audience, the meeting ran out of time and ended.

— 2 —

Second Address before the United Nations, Fourth Committee, 1972

This speech was given during Amilcar Cabral's last visit to the United States. Presented before the Twenty-Seventh Session of the Fourth Committee of the United Nations General Assembly in New York City, October 16, 1972, its contents were identified: "Questions of Territories under Portuguese Administration."

For the second time, I have the honor to address the Fourth Committee on behalf of the African people of Guinea and the Cape Verde Islands, whose sole, legitimate, and true representative is the PAIGC. I do so with gratification, being fully aware that the members of the Committee are our comrades in the difficult but inspiring struggle for the liberation of peoples and mankind, and against oppression of all kinds in the interest of a better life in a world of peace, security, and progress.

While not forgetting the often remarkable role that Utopia could play in furthering human progress, the PAIGC is very realistic. We know that, among members of the Fourth Committee, there are some who, perhaps in spite of themselves, are duty bound to adopt an obstructionist, if not negative, attitude when dealing with problems relating to the struggle for national liberation in Guinea and Cape Verde. I venture to say "in spite of themselves," because, leaving aside compelling reasons of State policy, it is difficult to believe that responsible men exist who fundamentally oppose the legitimate aspirations of the African people to live in dignity, freedom, national independence, and progress, because in the modern world, to support those who are suffering and fighting for their liberation, it is not necessary to be courageous; it is enough to be honest.

I addressed the Fourth Committee for the first time on 12 December 1962. Ten years is a long and even decisive period in the life of a human being, but a short interval in the history of a people. During that decade, sweeping, radical, and irreversible changes have occurred in the life of the people of Guinea and Cape Verde. Unfortunately, it is impossible for me to refresh the memory of the members of the Committee in order to compare the situation of those days with the present, because most, if not all, of the representatives in the Committee are not the same. I will therefore briefly recapitulate the events up to the present.

On 3 August 1959, at a crucial juncture in the history of the struggle, the Portuguese colonialists committed the massacre of Pidjiguiti, in which the dock workers of Bissau and the river transport strikers were the victims and which, at a cost of fifty killed and over one hundred strikers wounded, was a painful lesson for our people, who learned that there was no question of choosing between a peaceful struggle and armed combat; the Portuguese had weapons and were prepared to kill. At a secret meeting of the PAIGC leaders, held at Bissau on 19 September 1959, the decision was taken to suspend all peaceful representations to the authorities in the villages and to prepare for the armed struggle. For that purpose, it was necessary to have a solid political base in the countryside. After three years of active and intensive mobilization and organization of the rural populations, PAIGC managed to create that base in spite of the increasing vigilance of the colonial authorities.

Feeling the winds of change, the Portuguese colonialists launched an extensive campaign of police and military repression against the nationalist forces. In June 1962, over two thousand patriots were arrested throughout the country. Several villages were set on fire and their inhabitants massacred. Dozens of Africans were burnt alive or drowned in the rivers and others tortured. The policy of repression stiffened the people's determination to continue the fight. Some skirmishes broke out between the patriots and the forces of colonialist repression.

Faced with that situation, the patriots considered that only an appropriate and effective intervention by the United Nations in support of the inalienable rights of the people of Guinea and the Cape Verde Islands could induce the Portuguese Government to respect international morality and legality. In light of subsequent events, we might well be considered to have been naive. We believed it to be our duty and right to have recourse to the international Organization. In the circumstances, we considered it absolutely necessary to appeal to the Fourth Committee. Our message was the appeal of a people confronted with a particularly difficult situation but resolved to pay the price required to regain our dignity and freedom, as also proof of our trust in the strength of the principles and in the capacity for action of the United Nations.

What was the Fourth Committee told at that time? First of all, PAIGC clearly described the reasons for and purposes of its presence in the United Nations and explained that it had come as the representative of the African people of "Portuguese" Guinea and the Cape Verde Islands. The people had placed their entire trust in PAIGC, an organization that had mobilized and organized them for the struggle for national liberation. The people had been gagged by the total lack of fundamental freedoms and by the Portuguese colonial repression. They considered those who had defended their interest in every possible way throughout the preceding fifteen years of Africa's history to be their lawful representatives.

PAIGC had come to the Fourth Committee not to make propaganda or to extract resolutions condemning Portuguese colonialism, but to work with the Committee in order to arrive at a constructive solution of a problem, which was both that of the people of Guinea and Cape Verde and that of the United Nations itself: the immediate liberation of that people from the colonial yoke.

Nor had it come to inveigh against Portuguese colonialism, as had already been done many times—just as attacks had already been made and condemnations uttered against Portuguese colonialism, whose characteristics, subterfuges, methods, and activities were already more than well known to the United Nations and world opinion.

PAIGC had come to the Fourth Committee because of the situation actually prevailing in our country and with the backing of international law, in order to seek, together with the members of the Committee, including the Portuguese delegation, the shortest and most effective way of rapidly eliminating Portuguese colonialism from Guinea and the Cape Verde Islands. The time had come for our people and party to dispense with indecision and promises and to adopt definitive decisions and take specific action. We had already agreed to make great sacrifices and were determined to do much more to recover our liberty and human dignity, whatever the path to be followed.

It was not by chance that our presence on the Committee had not been considered indispensable until then. The legal, human, and material requisites for action had not existed. In the course of the preceding years, those requisites had been gradually accumulating, both for the United Nations and for the people engaged in the struggle, and PAIGC was convinced that the time had come to act and that the United Nations and the people of Guinea and Cape Verde could really do so. PAIGC thought that, in order to act, it was necessary to establish close and effective cooperation and that it had the right and duty to help the United Nations so that it, in its turn, could help it to win back national freedom and independence. The help that PAIGC could provide had been mainly specific information on the situation in our country, a clear definition of the position adopted, and the submission of specific proposals for a solution.

After describing the situation prevailing in the country, especially with regard to the intensified police and military repression, the fiction of the so-called reforms introduced by the Portuguese government in September 1961 and the future prospects for our struggle, PAIGC analyzed the problems relating to the legality or illegality of the struggle.

I will pass over some parts of that statement and confine myself to recalling that it was said that the resolution on decolonization not only imposed, on Portugal and the people of Guinea and Cape Verde, the obligation to end colonial domination in that country, but also committed the United Nations itself to take action in order to end colonial domination wherever it existed, with a view to facilitating the national independence of all colonial peoples. The people of Guinea and Cape Verde were convinced that the Portuguese government could not continue obstinately and with impunity to commit an international crime and that the United Nations had all the necessary means at its disposal for ordering and applying practical and effective measures designed to ensure respect for the principles of the Charter, impose international legality in our country, and defend the interests of peace and civilization.

The representatives of the people of Guinea and the Cape Verde Islands did not come to ask the United Nations to send troops to free our country from the Portuguese colonial yoke, because, even though it might have been able to do so, we did not think it necessary, as we were sure of our ability to liberate our own country. We invoked the right to the collaboration and practical assistance of the United Nations with a view to expediting the liberation of our country from the colonial yoke and thus reducing the human and material losses that a protracted struggle might entail.

PAIGC was aware, not only of the legality of our struggle, but also of the fact that, fighting as we had been by all the means at our disposal for the liberation of our country, we had also been defending international legality, peace, and the progress of mankind.

The struggle had ceased to be strictly national and had become international. In Guinea and Cape Verde the fight for progress and freedom from poverty, suffering, and oppression had been waged in various forms. While it was true that the victims of the fight had been the sons of the people of Guinea and Cape Verde, it was also true that each comrade who had succumbed to torture or had fallen under the bullets of the Portuguese colonialists was identified—through the hope and conviction that the people of our country cherished in their hearts and minds—with all peace-loving and freedom-loving men who wished to live a life of progress in the pursuit of happiness.

In our country the fight had been waged not only to fulfill aspirations for freedom and national independence but also—and it would be continued until victory was won—to ensure respect for the resolutions and Charter of the United Nations. In the prisons, towns, and fields of our country, a battle had been fought between the United Nations, which had demanded the elimination of the system of colonial domination of peoples, and the armed forces of the Portuguese government that had sought to perpetuate the system in defiance of the people's legitimate rights.

The question had risen as to who was actually engaged in the fight. When a fighter had succumbed in our country to police torture or had been murdered in prison or burnt alive or machine-gunned by the Portuguese troops, for what cause had he given his life?

He had given his life for the liberation of our people from the colonial yoke and hence for the cause of the United Nations. In fighting and dying for the country's liberation, he had given his life, in a context of international legality, for the ideals set forth in the Charter and resolutions of the United Nations, especially for the resolution on decolonization.

For our people, the only difference between an Indian soldier, an Italian pilot, or a Swedish official who had died in the Congo, and the combatant who had died in Guinea or the Cape Verde Islands was that the latter, fighting in his own country in the service of the same ideal, was no more than an anonymous combatant for the United Nations cause.

PAIGC believed that the time had come to take stock of the situation and make radical changes in it, since it benefited only the enemies of the United Nations and, more specifically, Portuguese colonialism.

We Africans, having rejected the idea of begging for freedom, which was contrary to our dignity and our sacred right to freedom and independence, reaffirmed our steadfast decision to end colonial domination of our country, no matter what the sacrifices involved, and to conquer for ourselves the opportunity to achieve in peace our own progress and happiness.

With that aim in view and on the basis of that irrevocable decision, PAIGC had defined three possible ways in which the conflict between the government of Portugal and the African people might evolve and be resolved. Those three possibilities were the following: (a) a radical change in the position of the Portuguese government; (b) immediate specific action by the United Nations; and (c) a struggle waged exclusively by the people with their own means.

As proof of its confidence in the organization, and in view of the influence that some of the latter's Members could certainly exert on the Portuguese government, PAIGC had taken into consideration only the first two possibilities, and in that connection had submitted the following specific proposals:

With regard to the first possibility:

- The immediate establishment of contact between the Portuguese delegation and the PAIGC delegation;
- Consultations with the Portuguese government to set an early date for the beginning of negotiations between that

government's representatives and the lawful representatives of Guinea and the Cape Verde Islands;
- Pending negotiations, suspension of repressive acts by the Portuguese colonial forces and of all actions by the nationalists.

With regard to the second possibility:

- Acceptance of the principle that United Nations assistance would not be really effective unless it was simultaneously moral, political, and material;
- Immediate establishment within the United Nations of a special committee for the self-determination and national independence of the Territories under Portuguese administration;
- Immediate commencement of that committee's work before the close of the General Assembly session.

PAIGC also stated that it was ready to cooperate fully with that committee and proposed that the latter should be entrusted with the task of giving concrete assistance to our people so that we could free ourselves speedily from the colonial yoke. Since those proposals were not favorably received by the Portuguese government or the United Nations, the patriotic forces of our country launched a general struggle against the colonialist forces in January 1963 in order to respond, by an armed struggle for liberation, to the colonial genocidal war unleashed against the people by the government of Portugal.

Almost ten years later, PAIGC is again appearing before the Fourth Committee. The situation is completely different, however, both within the country and at the international level. The Fourth Committee and the United Nations are now better informed than ever before about the situation. In addition to the current information (reports, information bulletins, war communiques, and other documents that PAIGC has sent to the United Nations), PAIGC has, in those ten years, appeared before the Decolonization Committee to describe the progress of the struggle and prospects for its future evolution. Dozens of filmmakers, journalists, politicians, scientists, writers, artists, photographers, and so on of various nationalities have visited the country on their own initiative and at the invitation of PAIGC and have provided unanimous and irrefutable testimony regarding the situation.

Others—very few in number—have done the same on the colonialist side at the invitation of the Portuguese authorities and, with few exceptions, their testimony has not completely satisfied those authorities. For example, there was the case of the team from the French radio and television organization that visited all the "overseas provinces," and whose film was rejected by the Lisbon government because of the part relating to Guinea and Cape Verde. That film was shown to the Security Council in Addis Ababa. Another case was that of the group of representatives of the people of the United States, headed by Representative Charles Diggs, whose report on their visit to the country merits careful study by the Committee and anyone else wishing to obtain reliable information on the situation. However, the United Nations has at its disposal information which is, in our view, even more valuable, namely the report of the Special Mission which, at the invitation of PAIGC and duly authorized by the General Assembly, visited the liberated regions of the country in April 1972. I am not, therefore, appearing before the Committee to remedy a lack of information.

Furthermore, the United Nations and world opinion are sufficiently well informed about the crimes against African people committed daily by the Portuguese colonialists. A number of victims of Portuguese police and military repression have testified before United Nations bodies, particularly the Commission on Human Rights. At the twenty-sixth session, two of my countrymen, one with third-degree napalm burns and the other with mutilated ears and obvious signs of torture, appeared before the Committee. Those who have visited my country, including members of the United Nations Special Mission, have been able to see the horrifying consequences of the criminal acts of the Portuguese colonialists against the people and the material goods that are the fruits of their labor. Unfortunately, the United Nations, like the African people, is well aware that condemnations and resolutions, no matter how great their moral and political value, will not compel the Portuguese government to put an end to its crime of *lèse-humanité* [aggrieved humanity]. Consequently, I am not appearing before the Committee in order to obtain more violent condemnations and resolutions against the Portuguese colonialists.

Nor am I urging that an appeal should be made to the allies of the government of Portugal to cease giving it political support and material, military, economic, and financial assistance, which are factors of primary importance in the continuation of the Portuguese colonial war against Africa, since that has already been done on many past occasions with no positive results. It should be noted, not without regret, that I was right in stating almost ten years previously that, in view of the facts concerning the Portuguese economy and the interests of the States allied to the government of Portugal, recommending or even demanding a diplomatic, economic, and military boycott would not be an effective means of helping the African people. Experience has shown, on the contrary, that acting or being forced to act as real enemies of the liberation and progress of the African peoples, the allies of the Portuguese government, and in particular some of the main NATO powers have not only increased their assistance to the Portuguese colonialists but have systematically avoided or even boycotted any cooperation with the United Nations majority, which is seeking to determine legally the political and other steps that might induce the government of Portugal to comply with the principles of the Organization and the resolutions of the General Assembly. It was not ten years before but in recent years that the government of Portugal has received from its allies the largest quantities of war material, jet aircraft, helicopters, gunboats, launches, and so on. It was in 1972, not 1962, that the government of Portugal received some $500 million in financial assistance from one of its principal allies. If States that call themselves champions of freedom and democracy and defenders of the "free world" and the cause of self-determination and independence of peoples thus persist in supporting and giving practical assistance to the most retrograde colonialism on Earth, they must have very good reasons, at least in their own view. Perhaps an effort should be made to understand them, even if their reasons are unavowed or unavowable. It is no doubt necessary to take a realistic approach and to stop dreaming and asking the impossible, for, as we Africans say, "only in stories is it possible to cross the river on the shoulders of the crocodile's friend."

I am appearing once more before the United Nations to try, as in the past, to obtain from the Organization practical and effective assistance for my struggling people. However, as I have already said and as everyone knows, the current situation is in every way very different from that obtaining in 1962, and the aid that the African people need is likewise different.

During almost ten years of armed struggle and of enormous efforts and sacrifices, almost three- quarters of the national territory has been freed from Portuguese colonial domination and two- thirds brought under effective control, which means in concrete terms that in most of the country, the people have a solid political organization—that of PAIGC—a developing administrative structure, a judicial structure, a new economy free from all exploitation of the people's labor, a variety of social and cultural services (health, hygiene, education) and other means of affirming their personality and their ability to shape their destiny and direct their own lives. They also have a military organization entirely composed of and led by sons of the people. The national forces, whose task is to attack the colonialist troops systematically wherever they might be, in order to complete the liberation of the country, like the local armed forces, which are responsible for the defense and security of the liberated areas, are now stronger than ever, tempered by almost ten years of struggle. That is proved by the colonialists' inability to recover even the smallest part of the liberated areas by their increasingly heavy losses, and by the people's ability to deal them increasingly heavy blows, even in the main urban centers such as Bissau, the capital, and Bafata, the country's second-largest town.

For the people of Guinea and Cape Verde and our national party, however, the greatest success of our struggle does not lie in the fact that we have fought victoriously against the Portuguese colonialist troops under extremely difficult conditions, but rather in the fact that, while we were fighting, we began to create all the aspects of a new life—political, administrative, economic, social, and cultural—in the liberated areas. It is, to be sure, still a very hard life, since it calls for great effort and sacrifice in the face of a genocidal colonial war, but it is a life full of beauty, for it is one of productive, efficient work, freedom, and democracy in which the people have regained their dignity. The nearly ten years of struggle have not only forged a new, strong African nation but also created a new man and a new woman, people possessing an awareness of their rights and duties, on the soil of the African fatherland. Indeed, the most important result of the struggle, which is at the same time its greatest strength, is the new awareness of the country's men, women, and children.

The people of Guinea and Cape Verde do not take any great pride in the fact that every day, because of circumstances created and imposed by the government of Portugal, an increasing number of young Portuguese are dying ingloriously before the withering fire of the freedom fighters. What fills us with pride is our ever-increasing national consciousness, our unity—now indestructible—that has been forged in war, the harmonious development and coexistence of the various cultures and ethnic groups, the schools, hospitals and health centers that are operating openly in spite of the bombs and the terrorist attacks of the Portuguese colonialists, the people's stores that are increasingly able to supply the needs of the population, the increase and qualitative improvement in agricultural production, and the beauty, pride, and dignity of our children and our women, who were the most exploited human beings in the country. We take pride in the fact that thousands of adults have been taught to read and write, that the rural inhabitants are receiving medicines that were never available to them before, that no fewer than 497 high- and middle-level civil servants and professional people have been trained, and that 495 young people are studying at higher, secondary, and vocational educational establishments in friendly European countries, while fifteen thousand children are attending 156 primary schools and five secondary boarding schools and semi-boarding schools, with a staff of 251 teachers. This is the greatest victory of the people of Guinea and Cape Verde over the Portuguese colonialists, for it is a victory over ignorance, fear and disease—evils imposed on the African inhabitants for more than a century by Portuguese colonialism.

It is also the clearest proof of the sovereignty enjoyed by the people of Guinea and Cape Verde, who are free and sovereign in the greatest part of our national territory. To defend and preserve that sovereignty and expand it throughout the entire national territory, both on the continent and on the islands, the people have not only their armed forces but also all the machinery of a State, which, under the leadership of the party, is growing stronger and consolidating itself day by day. Indeed, the position of the people of Guinea and Cape Verde has for some time been comparable to that of an independent State, part of whose national territory—namely, the urban centers—is occupied by foreign military forces. Proof of that is the fact that for some years the people have no longer been subject to economic exploitation by the Portuguese colonialists, since the latter are no longer able to exploit them. The people of Guinea and Cape Verde are all the more certain of gaining their freedom because of the fact that, both in the urban centers and in the occupied areas, the clandestine organization and political activities of the freedom fighters are more vigorous than ever.

There is no force capable of preventing the complete liberation of my people and the attainment of national independence by my country. Nothing can destroy the unity of the African people of Guinea and Cape Verde and our unshakable determination to free the entire national territory from the Portuguese colonial yoke and military occupation.

Confronted with that situation and that determination, what is the attitude of the Portuguese government? Up until the death of Salazar, whose outmoded ways of thinking made it impossible for him to conceive of granting even fictitious concessions to the Africans, there was talk only of radicalizing the colonial war. Salazar, who would repeat over and over to anyone willing to listen that "Africa does not exist" (an assertion that clearly reflected an insane racism but that also perfectly summed up the principles and practices that have always characterized Portuguese colonial policy), was, at his advanced age, unable to survive the affirmation of Africa's existence: the victorious armed resistance of the African peoples to the Portuguese colonial war. Salazar was nothing more than a fanatical believer in the doctrine of European superiority and African inferiority. As everyone knew, Africa was the sickness that killed Salazar.

Marcelo Caetano, his successor, is also a theoretician (professor of colonial law at the Lisbon School of Law) and a practical politician (Minister of Colonies for many years). Caetano, who claims that he "knows the blacks," has decided on a new policy which, in the sphere of social relationships, is to be that of a kind of master who holds out the hand of friendship to his "boy." Politically speaking, the new policy is, in its essence, nothing more than the old tactic of force and deceit, while outwardly it makes use of the arguments and even the actual words of the adversary in order to confuse him, while actually maintaining the same position. That is the difference between the Salazarism of Salazar and the neo-Salazarism of Caetano. The objective remains the same: to perpetuate white domination of the Black masses of Guinea and Cape Verde.

Caetano's new tactic, which the people refer to as "the policy of smiling and bloodshed," is merely one more result and success of the struggle being waged by the Africans. That fact has been noted by many who have visited the remaining occupied areas of Guinea and Cape Verde, including the American congressman Charles Diggs, and it is also understood by the people of the occupied areas who replied to the colonialists' demagogic concessions with the words "Djarama, PAIGC," that is, "Thank you, PAIGC." In spite of those concessions and the launching of a vast propaganda campaign, both in Africa and internationally, the new policy has failed. The people of the liberated areas are more united than ever around the national party, while those of the urban centers and the remaining occupied areas are supporting the party's struggle more strongly every day both in Guinea and Cape Verde. Hundreds of young people are leaving the urban centers, especially Bissau, to join the fight. There are increasing desertions from the so-called *unidades africanas*, many of whose members are being held prisoner by the colonial authorities.

Confronted with that situation, the colonialists are resorting to increased repression in the occupied areas, particularly the cities, and stepping up the bombings and terrorist attacks against the liberated areas. Having been forced to recognize that they cannot win the war, they now know that no stratagem can demoralize the people of those areas and that nothing can halt our advance towards complete liberation and independence. They are therefore making extensive use of the means available to them and attempting at all costs to destroy as many lives and as much property as they can. The colonialists are making increased use of napalm and are actively preparing to use toxic substances, herbicides, and defoliants, of which they have large supplies in Bissau, against the freedom fighters.

The Portuguese government's desperation is all the more understandable because of the fact that the peoples of Angola and Mozambique are succeeding in their struggle and that the people of Portugal are becoming more strongly opposed to the colonial wars every day. In spite of appearances, Portugal's economic, political, and social position is steadily deteriorating and the population declining, mainly because of the colonial wars. I wish to reaffirm my people's solidarity not only with the fraternal African peoples of Angola and Mozambique but also with the people of Portugal, whom my own people have never equated with Portuguese colonialism. My people are more convinced than ever that the struggle being waged in Guinea and Cape Verde and the complete liberation of that territory will be in the best interests of the people of Portugal, with whom we wish to establish and develop the best possible relations on the basis of cooperation, solidarity, and friendship, in order to promote genuine progress in my country once it wins its independence.

Although the Portuguese Government has persisted in its absurd, inhuman policy of colonial war for almost ten years, the United Nations has made a significant moral and political contribution to the progress of my people's liberation struggle. The resolutions proclaiming that it is legitimate to carry on that struggle by any means necessary, the appeal to Member States to extend all possible assistance to the African liberation movements, the recommendations to the specialized agencies to cooperate with those movements through the OAU [Organization of African Unity], the granting of hearings to their representatives at the Security Council meetings in Addis Ababa, the granting of observer status to certain liberation movements and, in my own case, the Special Mission's visit to my country and the recognition of my party by the Committee on Decolonization as the only legitimate, authentic representative of the people of Guinea and Cape Verde represented important assistance to those struggling peoples. We are grateful for the aid received, from the Committee on Decolonization and its dynamic Chairman, the Fourth Committee and, through it, the General Assembly and all Member States which are sympathetic to our cause.

Nevertheless, I do not feel that there is nothing more the United Nations can do to aid my people's struggle. I am convinced that the Organization can and must do more to hasten the end of the colonial war in my country and the complete liberation of my people. I have for that reason submitted specific proposals to the Security Council in Addis Ababa. Because of my confidence in the United Nations and in its ability to take action in the specific case of Guinea and Cape Verde, I am now submitting new proposals aimed at the establishment of closer, more effective cooperation between the Organization and the national party, which is the legitimate representative of the people of Guinea and Cape Verde. Before doing so, I would draw attention to some important events that have taken place in my country in recent months.

I will not speak about the successes achieved by the freedom fighters during the past year, although they have been significant ones. I will begin by referring to the United Nations Special Mission's visit to my country, which was made in April despite the terrorist aggression launched by the Portuguese colonialists against the liberated South in an effort to prevent the visit from taking place. A historic and unique landmark for the United Nations and the liberation movements, the visit was unquestionably a great victory for my people, but it was also one for the international organization and for mankind. It provided a new stimulus to the courage and determination of my people and their fighters, who were willing to make sacrifices in order to make it possible. While it is true that the findings of the Special Mission merely added more evidence of the same kind, as had been given by many unimpeachably reliable visitors, various professional persons, and nationalists, they nevertheless have special value and significance, since they are findings of the United Nations itself, made by an official mission duly authorized by the General Assembly and consisting of respected representatives of three Member States. I emphasize the great importance of the Special Mission's success, express my gratitude to the General Assembly for authorizing it, and to Ecuador, Sweden, and Tunisia for allowing their distinguished representatives, Mr. Horacio Sevilla

Borja, Mr. Folke Lofgren, and Mr. Kamel Belkhira, to participate in it, and again congratulate all the participants and Secretariat staff members on having performed with exemplary courage, determination, and conscientiousness the duties of a historic and profoundly humanitarian assignment in the service of the United Nations and of the people of Guinea and Cape Verde, and hence in the service of mankind.

Any action, regardless of its motives, is sterile unless it produces practical and concrete results. PAIGC's motive in inviting the United Nations to send a Special Mission to its country was not to prove the sovereignty of the people of Guinea over vast areas of the country, a fact which was already clear to everyone; instead, it deliberately tried to give the United Nations another specific basis for taking effective measures against Portuguese colonialism. That basis has been established by the success of the Special Mission; it seems just and essential to take full advantage of it, since PAIGC, like the Special Mission, is convinced that the political situation of the people of Guinea, including their legal situation, cannot remain as it has been in the past. PAIGC is also convinced that the United Nations will be able to implement the recommendations of the Special Mission and declares its readiness to extend whatever cooperation is needed to that end.

Like any important event, the Mission's success involved some amusing sidelights, such as the desperate and preposterous response expressed both orally and in writing by the Lisbon government. In that connection, I quote a proverb current among the people of Guinea, "A person who spits at the sun succeeds only in dirtying his own face."

Another important event is the establishment of the first National Assembly of the people of Guinea. Universal general elections have just been held by secret ballot in all the liberated areas for the purpose of forming regional councils and choosing the 120 representatives to the first National Assembly, 80 elected by the masses of the people and 40 chosen from among the members of the Party. The people of Guinea and PAIGC are firmly resolved to take full advantage of the establishment of our new organs of sovereignty. The National Assembly will proclaim the existence of the State of Guinea and give it an executive authority that will function within the country. In that connection, PAIGC is sure of the fraternal and active support of the independent African States and feels encouraged by the certainty that not only Africa but also the United Nations and all genuinely anti-colonialist States will fully appreciate the political and legal development of the situation in that African nation. In point of fact, at the present stage of the struggle, the government of Portugal neither can, nor should, represent the people of Guinea either in the United Nations or in any other international organization or agency, just as it can never represent it in the OAU.

For that reason, PAIGC is not raising the question of calling for the expulsion of Portugal from the United Nations or from any other international organization. The real question is whether or not the people of Guinea, who hold sovereignty over most of their national territory, and who have just formed their first National Assembly, which is going to proclaim the existence of its State, headed by an executive authority, have the right to become a member of the international community within the framework of its organizations, even though part of its country is occupied by foreign military forces. The real question before the people of Guinea, which has to be answered categorically, is whether the United Nations and all the anti-colonialist forces are prepared to strengthen their support and their moral, political, and material assistance to that African nation as their specific capabilities permit.

It is true that the war is still ravaging the country and that the people will have to continue making sacrifices to win the liberation of their homeland. That has already happened and is happening in other places to peoples who have a government of their own and a standing in international law. But it is also true that, thanks to international solidarity, more and more resources (and more effective ones) are becoming available to the people of Guinea, enabling them to deal harder blows to the Portuguese colonial troops, and that the people's determination and the valor and experience of our fighters are increasing day by day. The only reason why PAIGC does not trouble to declare that Portugal runs the risk of military defeat in Guinea is that Portugal has never had any chance of victory, and for that reason, too, the people of Guinea will continue to maintain our principles: Peace, a search for dialogue, and negotiation for the solution of our conflict with the government of Portugal.

In the Cape Verde Islands, where hunger again reigns, while the colonialists are intensifying their oppression because of PAIGC's political activity, PAIGC is determined to promote the struggle by all necessary means in order to free the African people completely from the colonial yoke. Above all, PAIGC denounces the despicable efforts of the government of Portugal to take advantage of the situation in the Islands by exporting workers to Portugal and other colonies in order to sap the people's strength and thus undermine our struggle. PAIGC wishes to reaffirm that, by reason of the community of blood, history, interests, and struggle between the peoples of Guinea and the Islands, it is determined to make whatever sacrifices are necessary in order to liberate the Cape Verde archipelago from Portuguese domination.

I call to the attention of the United Nations through the Fourth Committee, the following proposals, based on the practical realities of the life of the people of Guinea and on all the considerations I have just discussed:

1. Representations to the government of Portugal for the immediate start of negotiations between the representatives of that government and those of PAIGC. The program of those negotiations should be based on a search for the most appropriate and effective means for the early attainment of independence by the people of Guinea. If the government of Portugal responds favorably to that initiative, PAIGC might consider ways of taking into account the interests of Portugal in Guinea.

2. Immediate acceptance of PAIGC delegates, in the capacity of associate members or observers, in all the specialized agencies of the United Nations as the sole legitimate representatives of the people of Guinea, as is already true in the case of ECA [Economic Commission for Africa].
3. Development of practical assistance from the specialized agencies, particularly UNESCO, WHO, FAO, and UNICEF, to the people of Guinea, as a part of that country's national reconstruction. I hope that any undue legalistic or bureaucratic obstacles in that sphere can be overcome.
4. Moral and political support by the United Nations for all initiatives that the people of Guinea and the PAIGC have decided to adopt with a view to an early end of the Portuguese colonial war and to the achievement of that African country's independence in order that it might soon occupy its rightful place in the international community.

In the hope that those proposals will be given serious consideration, I strongly urge all Member States of the United Nations, in particular Portugal's allies, the Latin American countries, and especially Brazil, to understand Guinea's position and support that African people's legitimate aspirations to freedom, independence, and progress. The Latin American countries have had to fight for their independence. Portugal often cites the case of Brazil as an example in favor of its position, even though a struggle for independence has taken place in Brazil as well. Portugal itself gained its freedom through a fratricidal struggle; the people of Guinea, however, have no family ties with the people of Portugal.

I thank the African countries, the socialist countries, the Nordic countries, and all other countries and nongovernmental organizations, such as the World Council of Churches, the World Church Services, and the Rowntree Social Trust, which are helping Guinea in its struggle for liberation. At the same time, I do not believe that the attitude of States giving aid to Portugal reflects the feelings of most of their inhabitants. The people of Guinea are certain of final victory and hope to establish cooperative and peaceful relations with all peoples. I thank the Committee for its welcome and reaffirm that I am at its disposal at any time.

—3—

The Nationalist Movements of the Portuguese Colonies: Opening Address at the Conference of Nationalist Organizations of the Portuguese Colonies, Dar es Salaam, 1965

Dear comrades and friends: I am going to tell you very simply and as briefly as possible about our position, our situation, and, if you like, our options. A brief analysis we would like to make objectively and without passion. If we do not forget the historical perspectives of the major events in the life of humanity; if, while maintaining due respect for all philosophies, we do not forget that the world is the creation of man himself, then colonialism can be considered as the paralysis or deviation or even the halting of the history of one people in favor of the acceleration of the historical development of other peoples.

This is why, when speaking of Portuguese colonialism, we should not isolate it from the totality of the other phenomena that have characterized the life of humanity since the industrial revolution, from the rise of capitalism to the Second World War. This is why, when speaking of our struggle, we should not isolate it from the totality of the phenomena that have characterized the life of humanity, in particular in Africa since the Second World War.

I remember that period very well. We are getting old. I remember very well how some of us, still students, got together in Lisbon, influenced by the currents that were shaking the world, and began to discuss what could today be called the re-Africanization of our minds. Yes, some of those people are here in this hall. And that, dear friends, is a striking victory against the retrograde forces of Portuguese colonialism. You have among you here Agostinho Neto, Mario de Andrade, Marcelino Dos Santos; you have among you Vasco Cabral and Dr. Mondlane. All of us, in Lisbon, some permanently, others temporarily, began this march, this already long march towards the liberation of our peoples.

In the Second World War, millions of men, women, and children, millions of soldiers gave their lives for an ideal, an ideal of democracy, freedom, progress, and a just life for all men. Clearly, we know that the Second World War produced fundamental contradictions within the imperialist camp itself. But we also know that one of the fundamental objectives of that war started by Hitler and his horde was the destruction of the socialist camp about to be born.

We know too that, in the heart of every man fighting in that war, there was hope, the hope for a better world. It was that hope that touched us all, making us fighters for the freedom of our peoples. But we must state openly that, equally if not more so, it is the concrete conditions of the life of our peoples—misery, ignorance, suffering of every kind, the complete negation of our most elementary rights—that have dictated our firm position against Portuguese colonialism and, consequently, against all injustice in the world.

We had many meetings, we created many organizations. I am going to recall just one of those organizations: the Anti-Colonialist Movement, MAC.

One day we will publish the famous—for us, very famous and historic—manifesto of the MAC, in which you will certainly find the preface to our struggle, the general line of the struggle, which we are victoriously waging today against Portuguese colonialism. In any struggle, it is of fundamental importance to define clearly who we are, and who is the enemy. We, the peoples of the Portuguese colonies, are African peoples, of this Africa ensnared by imperialism and colonialism for decades and even, in some cases, for centuries. We are from the part of Africa that the imperialists call Black Africa. Yes, we are Black. But we are men like all other men. Our countries are economically backward. Our peoples are at a specific historical stage characterized by this backward condition of our economy. We must be conscious of this. We are African peoples, we have not invented many things, we do not possess today the special weapons that others possess, we have no big factories, we don't even have for our children the toys that other children have, but we do have our own hearts, our own heads, our own history. It is this history that the colonialists have taken from us. The colonialists usually say that it was they who brought us into history: Today we show that this is not so. They made us leave history, our history, to follow them, right at the back, to follow the progress of their history. Today, in taking up arms to liberate ourselves, in following the example of other peoples who have taken up arms to liberate themselves, we want to return to our history, on our own feet, by our own means and through our own sacrifices. We, peoples of Africa, who are fighting against Portuguese colonialism, have suffered under very special conditions, because, for the past forty years, we have been under the domination of a fascist regime.

Who is this enemy who dominates us, stubbornly scorning all laws, all international legality and morality? This enemy is not the Portuguese people, nor even Portugal itself: For us, fighting for the freedom of the Portuguese colonies, the enemy is Portuguese colonialism, represented by the colonial-fascist government of Portugal. But obviously a government is also to some extent the result of the historical, geographical, and economic conditions of the country it governs. Portugal is an economically backward country, in which about 50 percent of the population is illiterate; a country that you will find at the bottom of all the statistical tables of Europe. This is not the fault of the Portuguese people, who, at a certain time in history, showed their valor, their courage, and their capacity, and who even today possess capable sons, just sons, sons who also want to regain freedom and happiness for their people.

Portugal is a country in no position at all to dominate any other country. Portugal came to our countries, proclaiming that it came in the service of God and in the service of civilization. Today we reply with arms in our hands: Whichever God is with the Portuguese colonialists; whichever civilization the Portuguese colonialists represent, we are going to destroy them because we are going to destroy every sort of foreign domination in our countries.

I will not go into detail about the characteristics of Portuguese colonialism. The main characteristic of present-day Portuguese colonialism is a very simple fact: Portuguese colonialism, or if you prefer the Portuguese economic infrastructure, cannot allow itself the luxury of being neocolonialist. This enables us to understand the whole attitude, all the stubbornness of Portuguese colonialism towards our peoples. If Portugal was economically advanced, if Portugal could be classified as a developed country, we should surely not be at war with Portugal today.

Many people criticize Salazar and say bad things about him. He is a man like any other. He has many failings, he is a fascist, we hate him, but we are not fighting against Salazar; we are fighting against the Portuguese colonial system. We don't dream that, when Salazar disappears, Portuguese colonialism will disappear.

Our national liberation struggle has a great significance both for Africa and for the world. We are in the process of proving that peoples such as ours—economically backward, living sometimes almost naked in the bush, not knowing how to read or write, not having even the most elementary knowledge of modern technology—are capable, by means of their sacrifices and efforts, of beating an enemy who is not only more advanced from a technological point of view but also supported by the powerful forces of world imperialism. Thus, before the world and before Africa we ask: Were the Portuguese right when they claimed that we were uncivilized peoples, peoples without culture? We ask: What is the most striking manifestation of civilization and culture, if not that shown by a people who takes up arms to defend its right to life, to progress, to work, and to happiness?

We, the national liberation movements joined in the CONCP, should be conscious of the fact that our armed struggle is only one aspect of the general struggle of the oppressed peoples against imperialism, of man's struggle for dignity, freedom, and progress. We should consider ourselves as soldiers, often anonymous, but soldiers of humanity in the vast front of struggle in Africa today.

We must also define clearly our position in relation to our people, in relation to Africa, and in relation to the world. We of the CONCP are committed to our peoples, we are fighting for the complete liberation of our peoples, but we are not fighting simply in order to hoist a flag in our countries and to have a national anthem. We of the CONCP are fighting so that insults may no longer rule our countries, martyred and scorned for centuries, so that our peoples may never more be exploited by imperialists—not only by Europeans, not only by people with white skin, because we do not confuse exploitation or exploiters with the color of men's skins; we do not want any exploitation in our countries, not even by Black people. . . .

In Africa we are all for the complete liberation of the African continent from the colonial yoke, for we know that colonialism is an instrument of imperialism. So we want to see all manifestations of imperialism totally wiped out from the soil of Africa; in the CONCP we are fiercely opposed to neocolonialism, whatever its form. Our struggle is not only against Portuguese colonialism; in the framework of our struggle, we want to make the most effective contribution possible to the complete elimination of foreign domination in our continent.

In Africa we are for African unity, but we are for African unity in favor of the African peoples. We consider unity to be a means, not an end. Unity can reinforce and accelerate the reaching of ends, but we must not betray the end. That is why we are not in such a great hurry to achieve African unity. We know that it will come, step by step, as a result of the fruitful efforts of the African peoples. It will come at the service of Africa and of humanity. In the CONCP we are firmly convinced that making full use of the riches of our continent, of its human, moral, and cultural capacities, will contribute to creating a rich human species, which in turn will make a considerable contribution to humanity. But we do not want the dream of this end to betray in its achievement the interests of each African people. We, for example, in Guinea and Cabo Verde, openly declare in our Party's program that we are willing to join any African people, with only one condition: That the gains made by our people in the liberation struggle, the economic and social gains and the justice that we seek and are achieving little by little, should not be compromised by unity with other peoples. That is our only condition for unity.

In Africa, we are for an African policy that seeks to defend first and foremost the interests of the African peoples, of each African country, but also for a policy that does not, at any time, forget the interests of the world, of all humanity. We are for a policy of peace in Africa and of fraternal collaboration with all the peoples of the world.

On an international level, we in the CONCP practice a policy of nonalignment. But for us nonalignment does not mean turning one's back on the fundamental problems of humanity and of justice. Nonalignment for us means not aligning ourselves with blocs, not aligning ourselves with the decisions of others. We reserve the right to make our own decisions, and if by chance our choices and decisions coincide with those of others, that is not our fault.

We are for the policy of nonalignment, but we consider ourselves to be deeply committed to our people and committed to every just cause in the world. We see ourselves as part of a vast front of struggle for the good of humanity. You understand that we are struggling first and foremost for our own peoples. That is our task in this front of struggle. This involves the whole problem of solidarity. We in the CONCP are fiercely in solidarity with every just cause. That is why our hearts, in FRELIMO [Mozambique], in MPLA [Angola], in the PAIGC, in the CLSTP [São Tomé and Príncipe], in all the mass organizations affiliated to the CONCP, beat in unison with the hearts of our brothers in Vietnam who are giving us a shining example by facing the most shameful and unjustifiable aggression of the U.S. imperialists against the peaceful people of Vietnam. Our hearts are equally with our brothers in the Congo, who, in the bush of that vast and rich African country, are seeking to resolve their problems in the face of imperialist aggression and of the maneuvers of imperialism through their puppets. That is why we of the CONCP proclaim loud and clear that we are against Tshombe [Congolese Prime Minister], against all the Tshombes of Africa. Our hearts are also with our brothers in Cuba, who have shown that, even when surrounded by the sea, a people is capable of taking up arms and successfully defending its fundamental interests and of deciding its own destiny. We are with the Blacks of North America, we are with them in the streets of Los Angeles, and when they are deprived of all possibility of life, we suffer with them.

We are with the refugees, the martyred refugees of Palestine, who have been tricked and driven from their own homeland by the maneuvers of imperialism. We are on the side of the Palestinian refugees and we support wholeheartedly all that the sons of Palestine are doing to liberate their country, and we fully support the Arab and African countries in general in helping the Palestinian people to recover their dignity, their independence, and their right to live. We are also with the peoples of Southern Arabia, of so-called French Somaliland, of so-called Spanish Guinea, and we are also most seriously and painfully with our brothers in South Africa who are facing the most barbarous racial discrimination. We are absolutely certain that the development of the struggle in the Portuguese colonies, and the victory we are winning each day over Portuguese colonialism, is an effective contribution to the elimination of the vile, shameful regime of racial discrimination, of apartheid in South Africa. And we are also certain that peoples like that of Angola, that of Mozambique, and ourselves in Guinea and Cabo Verde, far from South Africa, will soon, very soon we hope, be able to play a very important role in the final elimination of that last bastion of imperialism and racism in Africa, South Africa.

We strongly support all just causes in the world, but we are also reinforced by the support of others. We receive concrete assistance from many people, from many friends, from many brothers. We accept every sort of assistance, from wherever it comes, but we never ask anybody for the assistance that we need. We just wait for whatever assistance each person or people can give to our struggle. Those are our ethics of assistance.

It is our duty to state here, loud and clear, that we have firm allies in the socialist countries. We know that all the African peoples are our brothers. Our struggle is their struggle. Every drop of blood that falls in our countries falls also from the body and heart of our brothers, these African peoples. But we also know that, since the socialist revolution and the events of the Second World War, the face of the world has been definitely changed. A socialist camp has arisen in the world. This has radically changed the balance of power, and this socialist camp is today showing itself fully conscious of its duties, international and historic, but not moral, since the peoples of the socialist countries have never exploited the colonized peoples. They are showing themselves conscious of their duty, and this is why I have the honor of telling you openly here that we are receiving substantial and effective aid from these countries, which is reinforcing the aid that we receive from our African brothers. If there are people who don't like to hear this, let them come and help us in our struggle, too. But they can be sure that we are proud of our own sovereignty.

And what are they doing, these people who don't like to hear us saying that the socialist countries are helping us? They are helping Portugal, the fascist-colonial government of Salazar. Everybody knows today that Portugal, the Portuguese government, if it could not count on the assistance of its NATO allies, would not be able to carry on fighting against us. But we must state clearly what NATO means. Yes, we know: NATO is a military bloc which defends the interests of the West, of Western civilization, etc. . . . That is not what we wish to discuss. NATO is concrete countries, concrete governments and states. NATO is the USA. We have captured in our country many U.S. weapons. NATO is the Federal Republic of Germany. We have a lot of Mauser rifles taken from Portuguese soldiers. NATO, for the time being at least, is France. In our country there are Alouette helicopters. NATO is, too, to a certain extent, the government of that heroic people who has given so many examples of love of freedom, the Italian people. Yes, we have captured from the Portuguese machine-guns and grenades made in Italy.

Portugal has other allies, too: South Africa, Mr. Smith of Southern Rhodesia, the government of Franco, and other obscure allies who hide their faces because of the shame this represents. But all this assistance that the Salazar government receives to kill our people and burn our villages in Angola, Mozambique, Guinea, Cabo Verde, and São Tomé has been incapable of stopping our national liberation struggle. On the contrary, our forces become stronger each day. And why? Because our strength is the strength of justice, progress, and history; and justice, progress, and history belong to the people. Because our fundamental strength is the strength of the people. It is our peoples who support our organizations. It is our peoples who are making sacrifices every day to supply all the needs of our struggle. It is our peoples who guarantee the future and the certainty of our victory.

In the perspective of our struggle, the place of this conference is clear. We must strengthen our unity, not only within each country but also among ourselves, as peoples of the Portuguese colonies. The CONCP has a very special significance for us. We have the same colonial past; we have all learned to speak and write Portuguese, but we have an even greater, and perhaps even more historic, strength: the fact that we began the struggle together. It is the struggle that makes comrades, that makes companions, for the present and for the future. The CONCP is for us a fundamental force in the struggle. The CONCP is in the heart of every fighter in our country, in Mozambique and Angola. The CONCP must also be an example, of which we are proud, to the peoples of Africa. Because, in this glorious struggle against imperialism and colonialism in Africa, we are the first colonies to have joined together to discuss together, to plan together, to study together the problems concerning the development of their struggle. This is surely a very interesting contribution to the history of Africa and to the history of our peoples.

Africa assists us, yes. There are some African countries which assist us as much as they can, directly, bilaterally. But in our opinion, Africa does not assist us enough. In our opinion, Africa could help us much more, if Africa could understand the value and importance of our struggle against Portuguese colonialism; so we hope that, [based] on the experience of the two years since Addis Ababa, the next summit conference of African heads-of-state will take concrete steps to effectively reinforce Africa's aid to the combatants of Guinea, Cabo Verde, Sãn Tomé, Mozambique, and Angola.

Equally, our friends in the world, and in particular our friends in the socialist countries, will surely be aware that the development of our struggle involves the development of their fraternal assistance; and we are sure that the socialist countries and the progressive forces of the West will develop their assistance and their political, moral, and material support for our struggle as this struggle itself develops.

To finish, I would like to simply say this: In our country, in Guinea and the Cabo Verde Islands, the colonialist troops are pulling further back each day. Today if we want to fight the colonialist troops, we have to go to them, we have to fight them in their barracks. But we must go there because we must eliminate Portuguese colonialism from our country. We are sure, dear friends, that it will soon be the same in Mozambique—and it is already happening in certain areas there. It will be the same in Angola—and it is already happening in Cabinda. The Portuguese colonialists are beginning to be afraid of us. They sense now that they are lost, but I assure you that if they were present here today—it's a pity they don't have any agents here—seeing us, hearing all the delegations speak, seeing all these people, seeing the fraternal welcome that the government of Tanzania has given us, the fear of the Portuguese colonialists would be even greater. But comrades and brothers, let us go forward, weapons in hand, everywhere where there is a Portuguese colonialist. Let us go forward and destroy him and liberate our countries quickly from the retrograde forces of Portuguese colonialism. But let us prepare ourselves, too, each day, and be vigilant, so as not to allow a new form of colonialism to be established in our countries; so as not to allow in our countries any form of imperialism; so as not to allow neocolonialism, already a cancerous growth in certain parts of Africa and of the world, to reach our own countries.

— 4 —

National Liberation and Culture

The Occasion and Context of the Text

Dr. Eduardo Mondlane, the first president of FRELIMO, the Mozambique Liberation Front, was assassinated by agents of Portuguese colonialism, in Dar es Salaam, Tanzania, on February 3, 1969. The following text is the inaugural Eduardo Mondlane Memorial Lecture delivered by Amilcar Cabral on February 20, 1970, at Syracuse University under the auspices of the Program of Eastern African Studies of the Maxwell School of Citizenship and Public Affairs. (It was translated from French by Maureen Webster.)

Shortly after the assassination of Dr. Eduardo Mondlane, the Program of Eastern African Studies established a memorial endowment to support an annual distinguished lecture series in Dr. Mondlane's memory. In a sense, Dr. Mondlane's academic home became Syracuse University, where he taught after receiving his doctorate in sociology from Northwestern University and working for the United Nations Secretariat. He subsequently returned to Africa with his wife and family to organize FRELIMO.

The Mondlane Lectureship is conceived as a series that seeks to embody Dr. Mondlane's rare combination of keen intellectual insight, political commitment, and warm humanism. While future Mondlane Memorial Lecturers were intended, quite appropriately, to include leaders of change from continents other than Africa, it was felt that no one could better inaugurate the Lectures than Amilcar Cabral.

Preface

It is a great honor to participate in this ceremony to pay homage to our companion in struggle and a worthy son of Africa, the mourned Dr. Eduardo Mondlane, former President of FRELIMO, assassinated in cowardly fashion by Portuguese colonialists and their allies on February 3, 1969, in Dar es Salaam.

We want to thank Syracuse University and particularly the Program of Eastern African Studies, directed by the scholar and teacher, Marshall Segall, for this initiative. It demonstrates, not only the respect and admiration you have for the unforgettable personality of Dr. Eduardo Mondlane, but also your solidarity with the heroic struggle of the Mozambican people and of all African peoples for national liberation and progress.

In accepting your invitation—which is considered as addressed to our people and to our fighters—we wanted once more to demonstrate our militant friendship and solidarity with the people of Mozambique and their beloved leader, Dr. Eduardo Mondlane, with whom we have been linked by fraternal bonds in the common struggle against the particularly retrograde Portuguese colonialism. Our friendship and our solidarity are all the more sincere in that we have not always agreed with our comrade Eduardo Mondlane, whose death was also a loss for our people.

Other speakers have had the opportunity to sketch the life of Dr. Eduardo Mondlane and to offer well-merited praise. We want quite simply to reaffirm our admiration for the African patriot and eminent man of culture that he was. We also wish to say that the great merit of Eduardo Mondlane did not lie in his decision to struggle for the freedom of his people. His principal merit lay in being able to merge himself with the reality of his country, to identify with his people, and to acculturate himself through the struggle that he directed with courage, determination, and wisdom.

Eduardo Chivambo Mondlane, African of rural background, son of peasants and a tribal chief, child educated by missionaries, Black pupil of the white schools of colonial Mozambique, university student in racist South Africa, young protégé of an American foundation, fellowship holder at an American university, Ph.D. from Northwestern University, high official in the United Nations, Professor at Syracuse University, President of the Mozambique Liberation Front, fallen in combat for the freedom of his people.

The life of Eduardo Mondlane is, indeed, singularly rich in experience. If one considers the short period when he was a trainee-worker in an agricultural enterprise, we can say that his life cycle includes, practically, all the categories of African colonial society: From the peasantry to the assimilated "petite bourgeoisie," and, on the cultural plane, from the village universe to a universal culture open to the world—its problems, its contradictions, and prospects for growth.

The important thing is that, after this long journey, Eduardo Mondlane was able to effect his return to the village, as a freedom fighter, and to stimulate the progress of his people, enriched by experiences (and how profound they were!) in the world today. Thus, he gave a potent example: Facing all the difficulties, fleeing the temptations, freeing himself from compromises of action or compromises of conscience, from cultural (hence political) alienation, he was able to confront his own roots, to identify with his people and to devote himself to the cause of their national and social liberation. That is why the colonialist-imperialists did not forgive him.

That is why, instead of limiting ourselves to the more or less important problems of the common struggle against Portuguese colonialism, we will center our lecture on an essential problem: the dependent and reciprocal relationships between the struggle for national liberation and culture.

If we succeed in convincing the fighters for African liberation and all those who are interested in the liberty and progress of African peoples of the decisive importance of this problem in the process of the struggle, we will have rendered significant homage to Eduardo Mondlane.

National Liberation and Culture

When Goebbels, the brain behind Nazi propaganda, heard culture being discussed, he brought out his revolver. That shows that the Nazis—who were and are the most tragic expression of imperialism and of its thirst for domination—even if they were all degenerates like Hitler, had a clear idea of the value of culture as a factor of resistance to foreign domination.

History teaches us that, in certain circumstances, it is very easy for the foreigner to impose his domination on a people. But it also teaches us that, whatever may be the material aspects of this domination, it can be maintained only by the permanent, organized repression of the cultural life of the people concerned. Implantation of foreign domination can be assured definitively only by the physical liquidation of a significant part of the dominated population.

In fact, to take up arms to dominate a people is, above all, to take up arms to destroy, or at least to neutralize, to paralyze, its cultural life. For, as long as there continues to exist a part of these people retaining their own cultural life, foreign domination cannot be sure of its perpetuation. At any moment, depending on internal and external factors determining the evolution of the society in question, cultural resistance (indestructible) may take on new forms (political, economic, armed) in order fully to contest foreign domination.

The ideal for foreign domination, whether imperialist or not, would be to choose: (1) either to liquidate practically all the population of the dominated country, thereby eliminating the possibilities for cultural resistance; (2) or to succeed in imposing itself without damage to the culture of the dominated people—that is, to harmonize the economic and political domination of these people with their cultural personality.

The first hypothesis implies genocide of the indigenous population and creates a void that empties foreign domination of its content and its object: the dominated people. The second hypothesis has not, until now, been confirmed by history. The broad experience of humankind allows us to postulate that it has no practical viability: it is not possible to harmonize the economic and political domination of a people, whatever may be the degree of their social development, with the preservation of their cultural personality.

In order to escape this choice—which may be called the dilemma of cultural resistance—imperialist colonial domination has tried to create theories that, in fact, are only gross formulations of racism, and which, in practice, are translated into a permanent state of siege of the indigenous populations on the basis of racist dictatorship (or democracy).

This, for example, is the case with the so-called theory of progressive assimilation of native populations, which turns out to be only a more or less violent attempt to deny the culture of the people in question. The utter failure of this "theory," implemented in practice by several colonial powers, including Portugal, is the most obvious proof of its lack of viability, if not of its inhuman character. It attains its highest degree of absurdity in the Portuguese case, where Salazar affirmed that Africa does not exist.

This is also the case with the so-called theory of apartheid, created, applied, and developed on the basis of the economic and political domination of the people of Southern Africa by a racist minority, with all the outrageous crimes against humanity that involves. The practice of apartheid takes the form of unrestrained exploitation of the labor force of the African masses, incarcerated and repressed in the largest concentration camp mankind has ever known.

These practical examples give a measure of the drama of foreign imperialist domination as it confronts the cultural reality of the dominated people. They also suggest the strong, dependent, and reciprocal relationships existing between the cultural situation and the economic (and political) situation in the behavior of human societies. In fact, culture is always in the life of a society (open or closed) the more or less conscious result of the economic and political activities of that society, the more or less dynamic expression of the kinds of relationships that prevail in that society, on the one hand between the human being (considered individually or collectively) and nature, and, on the other hand, among individuals, groups of individuals, social strata, or classes.

The value of culture as an element of resistance to foreign domination lies in the fact that culture is the vigorous manifestation on the ideological or idealist plane of the physical and historical reality of the society that is dominated or to be dominated. Culture is simultaneously the fruit of a people's history and a determinant of history, by the positive or negative influence that it exerts on the evolution of relationships between the human being and his/her environment, among human beings or groups of human beings within a society, as well as among different societies. Ignorance of this fact may explain the failure of several attempts at foreign domination—as well as the failure of some national liberation movements.

Let us examine the nature of national liberation. We shall consider this historical phenomenon in its contemporary context, that is, national liberation in opposition to imperialist domination. The latter is, as we know, distinct both in form and in content from preceding types of foreign domination (tribal, military-aristocratic, feudal, and capitalist domination in the free competition era).

The principal characteristic, common to every kind of imperialist domination, is the negation of the historical process of the dominated people by means of violently usurping the free operation of the process of development of the productive forces. Now, in any given society, the level of development of the productive forces and the system for the social utilization of these forces (the ownership system) determine the mode of production. In our opinion, the mode of production, whose contradictions are manifested with more or less intensity through the class struggle, is the principal factor in the history of any human group, the level of the productive forces being the true and permanent driving power of history.

For every society, for every group of people, considered as an evolving entity, the level of the productive forces indicates the stage of development of the society and of each of its components in relation to nature, its capacity to act or to react consciously in relation to nature. It indicates and conditions the type of material relationships (expressed objectively or subjectively) that exist between the human being and his environment. The mode of production, which represents, in every phase of history, the result of the unceasing search for a dynamic equilibrium between the level of the productive forces and the system of social utilization of these forces, indicates the stage of development of any given society and of each of its components in relation to itself and in relation to history. It also indicates and conditions the type of material relationships (expressed objectively or subjectively) that exist among the various elements or groups constituting the society in question. Relationships and types of relationships between the human being and nature, between the human being and her/his environment. Relationships and types of relationships among individuals or collective components of a society. To speak of these is to speak of history, but it is also to speak of culture.

Whatever may be the ideological or idealistic characteristics of cultural expression, culture is an essential element of the history of a people. Culture is, perhaps, the product of this history just as the flower is the product of a plant. Like history, or because it is history, culture has as its material base the level of the productive forces and the mode of production. Culture plunges its roots into the physical reality of the environmental humus in which it develops, and it reflects the organic nature of the society, which may be more or less influenced by external factors. History allows us to know the nature and extent of the imbalances and conflicts (economic, political, and social) that characterize the evolution of a society; culture allows us to know the dynamic syntheses which have been developed and established by social conscience to resolve these conflicts at each stage of its evolution, in the search for survival and progress.

Just as happens with the flower in a plant, in culture there lies the capacity (or the responsibility) for forming and fertilizing the seedling that will assure the continuity of history, at the same time assuring the prospects for evolution and progress of the society in question. Thus, it is understood that imperialist domination, by denying the historical development of the dominated people, necessarily also denies their cultural development. It is also understood why imperialist domination, like all other [forms of] foreign domination, for its own security, requires cultural oppression and the attempt at direct or indirect liquidation of the essential elements of the culture of the dominated people.

The study of the history of national liberation struggles shows that generally these struggles are preceded by an increase in expressions of culture, consolidated progressively into a successful or unsuccessful attempt to affirm the cultural personality of the dominated people, as a means of negating the oppressor culture. Whatever may be the conditions of a people's subjection to foreign domination, and whatever may be the influence of economic, political, and social factors in practicing this domination, it is generally within the culture that we find the seed of opposition, which leads to the structuring and development of the liberation movement.

In our opinion, the foundation for national liberation rests in the inalienable right of every people to have their own history, whatever formulations may be adopted at the level of international law. The objective of national liberation is, therefore, to reclaim the right, usurped by imperialist domination, namely: the liberation of the process of development of national productive forces. Therefore, national liberation takes place when, and only when, the national productive forces are completely free of all kinds of foreign domination. The liberation of productive forces, and consequently of the ability to determine the mode of production most appropriate to the evolution [or growth] of the liberated people, necessarily opens up new prospects for the cultural development of the society in question, by returning to that society all its capacity to create progress.

A people who free themselves from foreign domination will be free culturally only if, without complexes and without underestimating the importance of positive accretions from the oppressor and other cultures, they return to the upward paths of their own culture, which is nourished by the living reality of its environment, and which negates both harmful influences and any kind of subjection to foreign cultures. Thus, it may be seen that, if imperialist domination has the vital need to practice cultural oppression, national liberation is necessarily an act of culture.

On the basis of what has just been said, we may consider the national liberation movement as the organized political expression of the culture of the people who are undertaking the struggle. For this reason, those who lead the movement must have a clear idea of the value of culture in the framework of the struggle and must have a thorough knowledge of the people's culture, whatever may be their level of economic development.

In our time [that is, the '60s and '70s of the last century], it is common to affirm that all peoples have a culture. The time is past when, in an effort to perpetuate the domination of peoples, culture was considered an attribute of privileged peoples or nations, and when, out of either ignorance or malice, culture was confused with technical power, if not with skin color or the shape of one's eyes. The liberation movement, as representative and defender of the culture of the people, must be conscious of the fact that, whatever may be the material conditions of the society it represents, the society is the bearer and creator of culture. The liberation movement must furthermore embody the mass character, the popular character of the culture—which is not and never could be the privilege of one or of some sectors of the society.

In the thorough analysis of social structures, which every liberation movement should be capable of making in relation to the imperatives of the struggle, the cultural characteristics of each group in society have a place of prime importance. For, while the culture has a mass character, it is not uniform, it is not equally developed in all sectors of society. The attitude of each social group towards the liberation struggle is dictated by its economic interests, but it is also influenced profoundly by its culture. It may even be admitted that these differences in cultural levels explain differences in behavior towards the liberation movement on the part of individuals who belong to the same socio-economic group. It is at this point that culture reaches its full significance for each individual: understanding and integrating into his/her environment, identifying with fundamental problems and aspirations of the society, accepting of the possibility of change in the direction of progress.

In the specific conditions of our country—and we would say, of Africa—the horizontal and vertical distribution of levels of culture is somewhat complex. In fact, from villages to towns, from one ethnic group to another, from one age group to another, from the peasant to the workman or to the indigenous intellectual who is more or less assimilated, and, as we have said, even from individual to individual within the same social group, the quantitative and qualitative level of culture varies significantly. It is of prime importance for the liberation movement to take these facts into consideration.

In societies with a horizontal social structure, such as the Balante, for example, the distribution of cultural levels is more or less uniform, variations being linked uniquely to characteristics of individuals or of age groups. On the other hand, in societies with a vertical structure, such as the Fula, there are important variations from the top to the bottom of the social pyramid. These differences in social structure illustrate once more the close relationship between culture and economy, and also explain differences in the general or sectoral behavior of these two ethnic groups in relation to the liberation movement.

It is true that the multiplicity of social and ethnic groups complicates the effort to determine the role of culture in the liberation movement. But it is vital not to lose sight of the decisive importance of the class character of the culture in the development of the liberation struggle, even when class structure is or appears to be in embryonic stages of development.

The experience of colonial domination shows that, in the effort to perpetuate exploitation, the colonizer not only creates a system to repress the cultural life of the colonized people; he also provokes and develops the cultural alienation of a part of the population, either by so-called assimilation of indigenous people, or by creating a social gap between the indigenous elites and the popular masses. As a result of this process of dividing or of deepening the divisions in the society, it happens that a considerable part of the population, notably the urban or peasant "petite bourgeoisie," assimilates the colonizer's mentality, considers itself culturally superior to its own people, and ignores or looks down upon their cultural values. This situation, characteristic of the majority of colonized intellectuals, is consolidated by increases in the social privileges of the assimilated or alienated group with direct implications for the behavior of individuals in this group in relation to the liberation movement. A reconversion of minds—of mental sets—is thus indispensable to the true integration of people into the liberation movement. Such reconversion—re-Africanization, in our case—may take place before the struggle, but it is completed only during the course of the struggle, through daily contact with the popular masses in the communion of sacrifice required by the struggle.

However, we must take into account the fact that, faced with the prospect of political independence, the ambition and the opportunism from which the liberation movement generally suffers may bring into the struggle unconverted individuals. The latter, on the basis of their level of schooling, their scientific or technical knowledge, but without losing any of their social class biases, may attain the highest positions in the liberation movement. Vigilance is thus indispensable on the cultural as well as the political plane. For, in the liberation movement as elsewhere, all that glitters is not necessarily gold: political leaders—even the most famous—may be culturally alienated people.

But the social class characteristics of the culture are even more discernible in the behavior of privileged groups in rural areas, especially in the case of ethnic groups with a vertical social structure, where, nevertheless, assimilation or cultural alienation influences are nonexistent or practically nonexistent. This is the case, for example, with the Fula ruling class. Under colonial domination, the political authority of this class (traditional chiefs, noble families, religious leaders) is purely nominal, and the popular masses know that true authority lies with and is acted upon by colonial administrators. However, the ruling class preserves in essence its basic cultural authority over the masses, and this has very important political implications.

Recognizing this reality, the colonizer, who represses or inhibits significant cultural activity on the part of the masses at the base of the social pyramid, strengthens and protects the prestige and the cultural influence of the ruling class at the summit. The colonizer installs chiefs who support him and who are to some degree accepted by the masses; he gives these chiefs material privileges such as education for their eldest children, creates chiefdoms where they did not exist before, develops cordial relations with religious leaders, builds mosques, organizes journeys to Mecca, etc. And, above all, by means of the repressive organs of colonial administration, he guarantees economic and social privileges to the ruling class in their relations with the masses. All this does not make it impossible that, among these ruling classes, there may be individuals or groups of individuals who join the liberation movement, although less frequently than in the case of the assimilated "petite bourgeoisie." Several traditional and religious leaders join the struggle at the very beginning or during its development, making an enthusiastic contributions to the cause of liberation. But here again vigilance is indispensable: preserving deep down the cultural prejudices of their class, individuals in this category generally see in the liberation movement the only valid means, using the sacrifices of the masses, to eliminate colonial oppression of their own class and to reestablish in this way their complete political and cultural domination of the people.

In the general framework of contesting colonial imperialist domination and in the actual situation to which we refer, among the oppressor's most loyal allies are found some high officials and intellectuals of the liberal professions, assimilated people, and also a significant number of representatives of the ruling class from rural areas. This fact gives some measure of the influence (positive or negative) of culture and cultural prejudices in the problem of political choice when one is confronted with the liberation movement. It also illustrates the limits of this influence and the supremacy of the class factor in the behavior of the different social groups. The high official or the assimilated intellectual, characterized by total cultural alienation, identifies himself by political choice with the traditional or religious leader who has experienced no significant foreign cultural influences. For these two categories of people place above all principles or demands of a cultural nature—and against the aspirations of the people—their own economic and social privileges, their own class interests. That is a truth that the liberation movement cannot afford to ignore without risking betrayal of the economic, political, social, and cultural objectives of the struggle.

Without minimizing the positive contribution that privileged classes may bring to the struggle, the liberation movement must, on the cultural level just as on the political level, base its action in popular culture, whatever may be the diversity of levels of culture in the country. The cultural combat against colonial domination—the first phase of the liberation movement—can be planned efficiently only on the basis of the culture of the rural and urban working masses, including the nationalist (revolutionary) "petite bourgeoisie" who have been re-Africanized or who are ready for cultural reconversion. Whatever may be the complexity of this basic cultural panorama, the liberation movement must be capable of distinguishing within it the essential from the secondary, the positive from the negative, the progressive from the reactionary, in order to characterize the master line that defines progressively a national culture.

In order for culture to play the important role that falls to it in the framework of the liberation movement, the movement must be able to preserve the positive cultural values of every well-defined social group, of every category, and to achieve the confluence of these values in the service of the struggle, giving it a new dimension—the national dimension. Confronted with such a necessity, the liberation struggle is, above all, a struggle both for the preservation and survival of the cultural values of the people and for the harmonization and development of these values within a national framework.

The political and moral unity of the liberation movement and of the people it represents and directs, implies achieving the cultural unity of the social groups that are of key importance for the liberation struggle. This unity is achieved, on the one hand, by total identification with the environmental reality and with the fundamental problems and aspirations of the people; and, on the other hand, by the progressive cultural identification of the various social groups participating in the struggle. As it progresses, the liberation struggle must bring diverse interests into harmony, resolve contradictions, and define common objectives in the search for liberty and progress. The taking to heart of its objectives by large strata in the population, reflected in their determination in the face of difficulties and sacrifices, is a great political and moral victory. It is also a cultural achievement of decisive importance for the subsequent development and success [that is, victory] of the liberation movement.

The greater the differences between the culture of the dominated people and the culture of their oppressor, the more possible such a victory becomes. History proves that it is much less difficult to dominate and to continue dominating a people whose culture is similar or analogous to that of the conqueror. It could be contended that the failure of Napoleon, whatever may have been the economic and political motivations of his wars of conquest, resulted from his ignorance of this principle, or from his inability to limit his ambition to the domination of peoples whose culture was more or less similar to that of France. The same thing could be said about other ancient, modern, or contemporary empires.

One of the most serious errors, if not the most serious error, committed by colonial powers in Africa, may have been to ignore or underestimate the cultural strength of African peoples. This attitude is particularly clear in the case of Portuguese colonial domination, which has not been content with denying absolutely the existence of the cultural values of the African and his/her social position, but has persisted in forbidding him/her all kinds of political activity. The people of Portugal, who have not even enjoyed the wealth taken from African peoples by Portuguese colonialism, but the majority of whom have assimilated the imperial mentality of the country's ruling classes, are paying very dearly today, in three colonial wars, for the mistake of underestimating our cultural reality.

The political and armed resistance of the people of the Portuguese colonies, as of other countries or regions of Africa, was crushed by the technical superiority of the imperialist conqueror, with the complicity of or betrayal by some indigenous ruling classes. Those elites who were loyal to the history and to the culture of the people were destroyed. Entire populations were massacred. The colonial kingdom was established with all the crimes and exploitation that characterize it. But the cultural resistance of the African people was not destroyed. Repressed, persecuted, betrayed by some social groups who were in league with the colonialists, African culture survived all the storms, taking refuge in the villages, in the forests, and in the spirit of the generations who were victims of colonialism. Like the seed that long awaits conditions favorable to germination in order to assure the survival of the species and its development, the culture of African peoples flourishes again today, across the continent, in struggles for national liberation. Whatever may be the forms of these struggles, their successes or failures, and the length of their development, they mark the beginning of a new era in the history of the continent and are both in form and in content the most important cultural element in the life of African peoples. The freedom struggle of African peoples is both the fruit and the proof of cultural vigor, opening up new prospects for the development of culture in the service of progress.

The time is past when it was necessary to seek arguments to prove the cultural maturity of African peoples. The irrationality of the racist "theories" of a Gobineau [reactionary French aristocrat, promoted a bogus "scientific" racism] or a Lévy-Bruhl [racist French philosopher and anthropologist] neither interests nor convinces anyone but racists. In spite of colonial domination (and perhaps even because of this domination), Africa was able to impose respect for her cultural values. She even showed herself to be one of the richest of continents in cultural values. From Carthage or Giza to Zimbabwe, from Meroe to Benin and Ife, from the Sahara or Timbuktu to Kilwa, across the immensity and the diversity of the continent's natural conditions, the culture of African peoples is an undeniable reality: in works of art as well as in oral and written traditions, in cosmological conceptions as well as in music and dance, in religions and beliefs as well as in the dynamic balance of economic, political, and social structures created by African humanity.

The universal value of African culture is now an incontestable fact. Nevertheless, it should not be forgotten that African humanity, whose hands, as the poet said, "placed the stones of the foundations of the world," has developed culture frequently, if not constantly, in adverse conditions: from deserts to equatorial forests, from coastal marshes to the banks of great rivers subject to frequent flooding, in spite of all sorts of difficulties, including plagues that have destroyed plants, animals, and humans alike. In agreement with Basil Davidson and other researchers in African history and culture, we can say that the accomplishments of the African genius in economic, political, social, and cultural domains, despite the inhospitable character of the environment, are epic—comparable to the major historical examples of the greatness of humankind.

Of course, this reality constitutes a reason for pride and a stimulus to those who fight for the liberation and the progress of African peoples. But it is important not to lose sight of the fact that no culture is a perfect, finished whole. Culture, like history, is an expanding and developing phenomenon. Even more important, we must take account of the fact that the fundamental characteristic of a culture is the highly dependent and reciprocal nature of its linkages with the social and economic reality of the environment, with the level of productive forces and the mode of production of the society that created it.

Culture, the fruit of history, reflects at every moment the material and spiritual reality of society, of the human-individual and of the human-social-being, faced with conflicts that set him/her against nature and the exigencies of a common life. From this we see that all culture is composed of essential and secondary elements, of strengths and weaknesses, of virtues and failings, of positive and negative aspects, of factors of progress and factors of stagnation or regression. From this also we can see that culture—the creation of society and the synthesis of the balances and solutions that society engenders to resolve the conflicts that characterize each phase of its history—is a social reality, independent of the will of men, the color of their skins, or the shape of their eyes.

A thorough analysis of cultural reality does not permit the claim that there exist continental or racial cultures. This is because, as with history, the development of culture proceeds in uneven fashion, whether at the level of a continent, a "race," or even a society. The coordinates of culture, like those of any developing phenomenon, vary in space and time, whether they be material (physical) or human (biological and social). The fact of recognizing the existence of common and particular features in the cultures of African peoples, independent of the color of their skin, does not necessarily imply that one and only one culture exists on the continent. In the same way that, from an economic and political viewpoint we can recognize the existence of several Africas, so also there are many African cultures.

Without any doubt, underestimation of the cultural values of African peoples, based upon racist feelings and upon the intention of perpetuating foreign exploitation of Africans, has done much harm to Africa. But in the face of the vital need for progress, the following attitudes or behaviors will be no less harmful to Africa: indiscriminate compliments; systematic exaltation of virtues without condemning faults; blind acceptance of the values of the culture, without considering what presently or potentially regressive elements it contains; confusion between what is the expression of an objective and material historical reality and what appears to be a creation of the mind or the product of a peculiar temperament; absurd linking of artistic creations, whether good or not, with supposed racial characteristics; and, finally, the non-scientific or a-scientific critical appreciation of cultural phenomena.

Thus, the important thing is not to lose time in more or less idle discussion of the specific or unspecific characteristics of African cultural values, but rather to look upon these values as a conquest of a small piece of humanity for the common heritage of humanity, achieved in one or several phases of its evolution. The important thing is to proceed to a critical analysis of African cultures in relation to the liberation movement and to the exigencies of progress—confronting this new stage in African history. It is important to be conscious of the value of African cultures in the framework of universal civilization, to compare this value with that of other cultures, not with a view to deciding its superiority or inferiority, but in order to determine, in the general framework of the struggle for progress, what contribution African culture has made and can make, and what are the contributions it can or must receive from elsewhere.

The liberation movement must, as we have said, base its action upon thorough knowledge of the culture of the people and be able to appreciate at their true value the elements of this culture, as well as the different levels that it reaches in each social group. The movement must also be able to discern in the entire set of cultural values of the people the essential and the secondary, the positive and the negative, the progressive and the reactionary, the strengths and the weaknesses. All this is necessary as a function of the demands of the struggle and in order to be able to concentrate action on what is essential without forgetting what is secondary, to induce the development of positive and progressive elements, and to combat flexibly, but with rigor, the negative and reactionary elements; and finally, in order to utilize strengths efficiently and to eliminate weaknesses or to transform them into strengths.

The more one realizes that the chief goal of the liberation movement goes beyond the achievement of political independence to the superior level of complete liberation of the productive forces and the construction of economic, social, and cultural progress of the people, the more evident is the necessity of undertaking a selective analysis of the values of the culture within the framework of the struggle for liberation. Now, the negative values of culture are generally an obstacle to the development of the struggle and to the building of this progress. The need for such an analysis of cultural values becomes more acute when, in order to face colonial violence, the liberation movement must mobilize and organize the people, under the direction of a strong and disciplined political organization, in order to resort to violence in the cause of freedom—the armed struggle for national liberation.

In this perspective, the liberation movement must be able, beyond the analysis mentioned above, to achieve gradually but surely as its political action develops the confluence of the levels of culture of the different social groups available for the struggle. The movement must be able to transform them into the national cultural force that undergirds and conditions the development of the armed struggle. It should be noted that the analysis of cultural reality already gives a measure of the strengths and weaknesses of the people when confronted with the demands of the struggle, and therefore represents a valuable contribution to the strategy and tactics to be followed, on the political as well as on the military plane. But only during the struggle, launched from a satisfactory base of political and moral unity, is the complexity of cultural problems raised in all its dimensions. This frequently requires successive adaptations of strategy and tactics to the realities that only the struggle is capable of revealing. Experience of the struggle shows how Utopian and absurd it is to profess to apply without considering local reality (and especially cultural reality) plans of action developed by other peoples during their liberation struggles and to apply solutions that they found to the problems with which they were or are confronted.

It can be said that, at the outset of the struggle, whatever may have been the extent of preparation undertaken, both the leadership of the liberation movement and the militant and popular masses have no clear awareness of the strong influence of cultural values in the development of the struggle, the possibilities culture creates, the limits it imposes, and above all how and how much culture is for the people an inexhaustible source of courage, of material and moral support, of physical and psychic energy that enables them to accept sacrifices—even to accomplish "miracles." But equally, in some respects, culture is very much a source of obstacles and difficulties, of erroneous conceptions about reality, of deviations in carrying out duties, and of limitations on the tempo and efficiency of a struggle that is confronted with the political, technical, and the scientific requirements of a war.

The armed struggle for liberation launched in response to the colonialist oppressor turns out to be a painful but efficient instrument for developing the cultural level of both the leadership strata in the liberation movement and the various social groups that participate in the struggle.

The leaders of the liberation movement, drawn generally from the "petite bourgeoisie" (intellectuals, clerks) or the urban working classes (workers, chauffeurs, salary-earners in general) who, having to live day by day with the various peasant groups in the heart of rural populations, come to know the people better. They discover at the grassroots the richness of their cultural values (philosophic, political, artistic, social, and moral), acquire a clearer understanding of the economic realities of the country, of the problems, sufferings, and hopes of the popular masses. The leaders realize, not without a certain astonishment, the richness of spirit, the capacity for reasoned discussion and clear exposition of ideas, the facility for understanding and assimilating concepts on the part of population groups that yesterday were forgotten, if not despised, and that were considered incompetent by the colonizer and even by some nationals. The leaders thus enrich their culture—develop personally and free themselves from complexes, reinforcing their capacity to serve the movement in the service of the people.

On their side, the working masses and, in particular, the peasants, who are usually illiterate and never have moved beyond the boundaries of their village or region, in contact with other groups lose the complexes which constrained them in their relationships with other ethnic and social groups. They realize their crucial role in the struggle; they break the bonds of the village universe to integrate progressively into the country and the world; they acquire an infinite amount of new knowledge, useful for their immediate and future activity within the framework of the struggle; and they strengthen their political awareness by assimilating the principles of national and social revolution postulated by the struggle. They thereby become more able to play the decisive role of providing the principal force behind the liberation movement.

As we know, the armed liberation struggle requires the mobilization and organization of a significant majority of the population, the political and moral unity of the various social classes, the efficient use of modern arms and of other means of war, the progressive liquidation of the remnants of tribal mentality, and the rejection of social and religious rules and taboos that inhibit development of the struggle (gerontocracies, nepotism, social inferiority of women, rites and practices that are incompatible with the rational and national character of the struggle, etc.). The struggle brings about other profound modifications in the life of populations. The armed liberation struggle implies, therefore, a veritable forced march along the road to cultural progress.

Consider these features inherent in an armed liberation struggle: the practice of democracy, of criticism and self-criticism, the increasing responsibility of populations for the direction of their lives, literacy work, creation of schools and health services, training of cadres from peasant and worker backgrounds—and many other achievements. When we consider these features, we see that the armed liberation struggle is not only a product of culture but also a determinant of culture. This is without a doubt for the people the prime recompense for the efforts and sacrifices that war demands. In this perspective, it behooves the liberation movement to define clearly the objectives of cultural resistance as an integral and determining part of the struggle.

From all that has just been said, it can be concluded that in the framework of the conquest of national independence and in the perspective of developing the economic and social progress of the people, these objectives must be at least the following: Development of a popular culture and of all positive indigenous cultural values; development of a national culture based upon the history and the achievements of the struggle itself; constant promotion of the political and moral awareness of the people (of all social groups) as well as of patriotism, of the spirit of sacrifice and devotion to the cause of independence, of justice, and of progress; development of a technical, technological, and scientific culture, compatible with the requirements for progress; development, on the basis of a critical assimilation of human achievements in the domains of art, science, literature, etc., of a universal culture for perfect integration into the contemporary world, in the perspectives of its evolution; constant and generalized promotion of feelings of humanism, of solidarity, of respect, and disinterested devotion to human beings.

The achievement of these objectives is indeed possible because the armed struggle for liberation, in the concrete conditions of life of African peoples, confronted with the imperialist challenge, is an act of insemination upon history—the major expression of our culture and of our Africanness. In the moment of victory, it must be translated into a significant leap forward of the culture of the people who are liberating themselves.

If that does not happen, then the efforts and sacrifices accepted during the struggle will have been made in vain. The struggle will have failed to achieve its objectives, and the people will have missed an opportunity for progress in the general framework of history.

Closing Remarks

Ladies and gentlemen, in celebrating by this ceremony the memory of Dr. Eduardo Mondlane, we pay homage to the politician, to the freedom fighter, and, especially, to a man of culture. Culture acquired not only during the course of his personal life and in the halls of the university, but culture acquired mainly in the midst of his people, in the course of the struggle for the liberation of his people.

It may be said that Eduardo Mondlane was barbarously assassinated because he was able to identify himself with the culture of his people, with their deepest aspirations, in spite of all the attempts or the temptations to alienate his African and Mozambican personality. Because he forged himself a new culture in the liberation struggle, he fell as a combatant. It is obviously easy to accuse the Portuguese colonialists and the agents of imperialism, their allies, of the abominable crime committed against the person of Eduardo Mondlane, against the people of Mozambique and against Africa. They were the ones who, in cowardly fashion, assassinated him. However, all men of culture, all those who fight for freedom, all spirits afire for peace and progress—all the enemies of colonialism and racism—must have the courage to take upon their shoulders their share of the responsibility for this tragic death. For, if Portuguese colonialism and imperialist agents can still liquidate with impunity a man like Dr. Eduardo Mondlane, it is because there is something rotten in the heart of humanity: imperialist domination. It is because human beings of good will, defenders of the culture of peoples, have not yet accomplished their duty on this planet.

In our opinion, this is the measure of the responsibility of those who listen to us in this temple of culture, in relation to the movement for liberation of oppressed peoples.

Soldiers inside a liberated zone. (LIBERATION NEWS SERVICE)

A PAIGC soldier studying. (LIBERATION NEWS SERVICE)

Soldiers at a military base in a liberated region of Guinea.
(LIBERATION NEWS SERVICE)

Students at a gymnasium class at the Aerolino Lopez Cruz boarding school located in the Cubucare Sector, Southern Zone, in Liberated Guinea. The school was named after the teacher who died while protecting the students during a Portuguese air raid in 1965. (UN PHOTO: YUTAKA NAGATA)

Members of the PAIGC being inspected by an officer in the Cubucare Sector.
(UN PHOTO: YUTAKA NAGATA)

On September 24, 1973, the Republic of Guinea-Bissau was proclaimed. Some of the political leaders of the Republic are seen here at a meeting: (far left) Chico Mendes, Prime Minister; (center) Luis Cabral, President of the Council of State; (right) Lucio Soares, commander of the Northern Front. (AIS: ROBERT VAN LIEROP)

Kitchen of a military encampment in a liberated zone.
(LIBERATION NEWS SERVICE)

Local military and political leaders meet at the office at a military encampment.
(LIBERATION NEWS SERVICE)

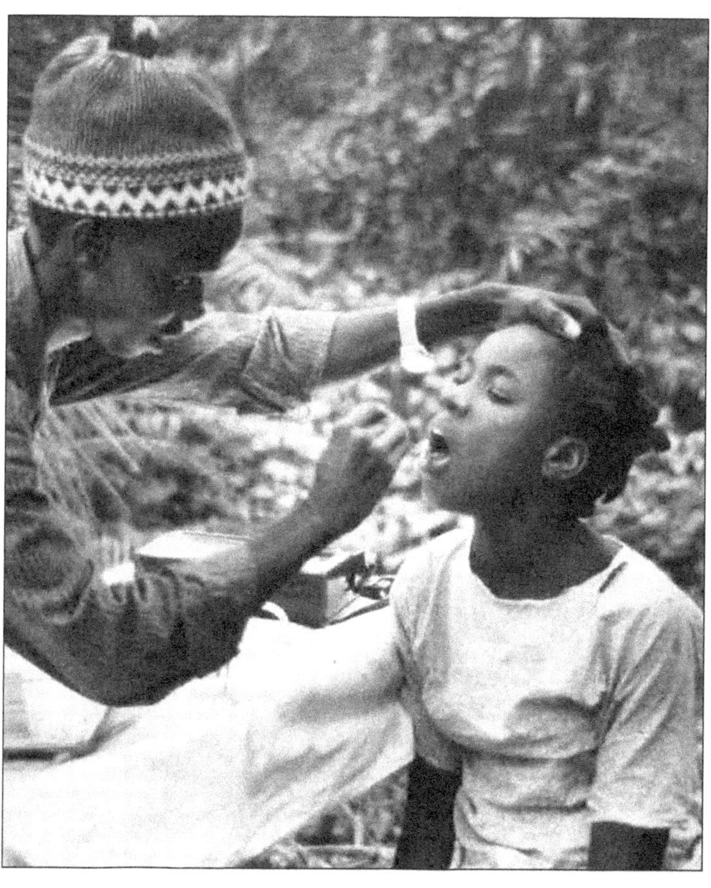

A young girl is examined by a nurse at a health station near the village of Bcama. (AIS: ROBERT VAN LIEROP)

Inside liberated Guinea. (PAIGC)

Mother and child listening to an address by a member of the 1972 Special Mission of the UN to liberated Guinea. (UN PHOTO: YUTAKA NAGATA)

Two PAIGC members taking a rest in the Balana-Kitafine Sector, liberated Guinea. (UN PHOTO: YUTAKA NAGATA)

Inside a liberated zone. (PAIGC)

Amilcar Cabral addressing an audience at Lincoln University where he received an honorary doctorate during his last visit to the United States, October 1972.

(AIS: RAY LEWIS)

A boy sits in front of UN and OAU representatives at a memorial service for Amilcar Cabral. Harlem, New York, January 24, 1973.

(UN PHOTO: YUTAKA NAGATA)

Lai Seck, in charge of Security in the Cubucare Sector. (UN PHOTO: YUTAKA NAGATA)

Paula Cassama, member of an action committee, addresses a mass meeting. The local action committees are composed of five members, two of whom must be women. (AIS: ROBERT VAN LIEROP)

A third grade student in a math class at the Aerolino Lopez Cruz boarding school. At right is Sevilla-Borza, chairman of the 1973 Mission of the United Nations to the liberated Guinea. (UN PHOTO: YUTAKA NAGATA)

People of the Cubucare Sector. (UN PHOTO: YUTAKA NAGATA)

— 5 —

Brief Analysis of the Social Structure in Guinea

Condensed text of a seminar held in the Frantz Fanon Centre in Treviglio, Milan, from May 1–3, 1964

I should like to tell you something about the situation in our country, "Portuguese" Guinea, beginning with an analysis of the social situation that has served as the basis for our struggle for national liberation. I shall make a distinction between the rural areas and the towns, or rather the urban centers, not that these are to be considered mutually opposed.

In the rural areas we have found it necessary to distinguish between two distinct groups: on the one hand, the group that we consider semi-feudal, represented by the Fulas, and, on the other hand, the group that we consider, so to speak, without any defined form of state organization, represented by the Balantes. There are a number of intermediary positions between these two extreme ethnic groups (as regards the social situation). I should like to point out straight away that, although in general, the semi-feudal groups were Muslim and the groups without any form of state organizations were animist, there was one ethnic group among the animists, the Mandjacks, that had forms of social relations that could be considered feudal at the time when the Portuguese came to Guinea.

I should now like to give you a quick idea of the social stratification among the Fulas. We consider that the chiefs, the nobles, and the religious figures form one group; after them come the artisans and the Dyulas, who are itinerant traders, and then after that come the peasants, properly speaking. I don't want to give a very thorough analysis of the economic situation of each of these groups now, but I would like to say that, although certain traditions concerning collective ownership of the land have been preserved, the chiefs and their entourages have retained considerable privileges as regards ownership of land and the utilization of other people's labor; this means that the peasants who depend on the chiefs are obliged to work for these chiefs for a certain period of each year. The artisans, whether blacksmiths (which is the lowest occupation) or leather-workers or whatever, play an extremely important role in the socioeconomic life of the Fulas and represent what you might call the embryo of industry. The Dyulas, whom some people consider should be placed above the artisans, do not really have such importance among the Fulas; they are the people who have the potential—which they sometimes realize—of accumulating money. In general, the peasants have no rights, and they are the really exploited group in Fula society.

Apart from the question of ownership and property, there is another element that it is extremely interesting to compare, and that is the position of women. Among the Fulas women have no rights; they take part in production, but they do not own what they produce. Besides, polygamy is a highly respected institution and women are, to a certain extent, considered the property of their husbands.

Among the Balantes, who are at the opposite extreme, we find a society without any social stratification; there is just a council of elders in each village or group of villages that decides on the day-to-day problems. In the Balante group, property and land are considered to belong to the village, but each family receives the amount of land needed to ensure subsistence for itself, and the means of production, or rather the instruments of production, are not collective but are owned by families or individuals.

The position of women must also be mentioned when talking about the Balantes. The Balantes still retain certain tendencies towards polygamy, although it is mainly a monogamous society. Among the Balantes, women participate in production but they own what they produce and this gives Balante women a position that we consider privileged, as they are fairly free; the only point on which they are not free is that children belong to the head of the family and the head of the family, the husband, always claims any children his wife may have. This is obviously to be explained by the actual economy of the group where a family's strength is ultimately represented by the number of hands there are to cultivate the land.

As I have said, there are a number of intermediate positions between these two extremes. In the rural areas I should mention the small African farm owners; this is a numerically small group but, all the same, it has a certain importance and has proved to be highly active in the national liberation struggle. In the towns (I shall not talk about the presence of Europeans in the rural areas, as there are none in Guinea) we must first distinguish between the Europeans and the Africans. The Europeans can easily be classified as they retain in Guinea the social stratification of Portugal (obviously depending on the function they exercise in Guinea). In the first place, there are the high officials and the managers of enterprises who form a stratum with practically no contact with the other European strata. After that there are the medium officials, the small European traders, the people employed in commerce, and the members of the liberal professions. After that come the workers, who are mainly skilled workers.

Among the Africans we find the higher officials, the middle officials, and the members of the liberal professions forming a group; then come the petit officials, those employed in commerce with a contract, who are to be distinguished from those employed in commerce without a contract, who can be fired at any moment. The small farm owners also fall into this group; by assimilation we call all these members of the African petite bourgeoisie (obviously, if we were to make a more thorough analysis, the higher African officials as well as the middle officials and the members of the liberal professions should also be included in the petite bourgeoisie). Next come the wage-earners (whom we define as those employed in commerce without any contract); among these, there are certain important subgroups such as the dock-workers, the people employed on the boats carrying goods and agricultural produce; there are also the domestic servants, who are mostly men in Guinea; there are the people working in repair shops and small factories, and there are also the people who work in shops as porters and suchlike—these all come under the heading of wage-earners. You will notice that we are careful not to call these groups the proletariat or working class.

There is another group of people whom we call the déclassés, in which there are two subgroups to be distinguished. The first subgroup is easy to identify—it is what would be called the lumpenproletariat if there was a real proletariat; it consists of really déclassé people, such as beggars, prostitutes, and so on. The other group is not really made up of déclassé people, but we have not yet found the exact term for it; it is a group to which we have paid a lot of attention, and it has proved to be extremely important in the national liberation struggle. It is mostly made up of young people who are connected to petit bourgeois or workers' families, who have recently arrived from the rural areas and generally do not work; they thus have close relations with the rural areas, as well as with the towns (and even with the Europeans). They sometimes live off one kind of work or another, but they generally live at the expense of their families. Here I should just like to point out a difference between Europe and Africa; in Africa there is a tradition that requires that, for example, if I have an uncle living in the town, I can come in and live in his house without working and he will feed me and house me. This creates a certain stratum of people who experience urban life and who can, as we shall see, play a very important role.

That is a very brief analysis of the general situation in Guinea, but you will understand that this analysis has no value unless it is related to the actual struggle. In outline, the methodological approach we have used has been as follows: First, the position of each group must be defined—to what extent and in what way does each group depend on the colonial regime? Next, we have to see what position they adopt towards the national liberation struggle. Then, we have to study their nationalist capacity, and lastly, envisaging the post-independence period, their revolutionary capacity.

Among the Fulas, the first group—the chiefs and their entourages—are tied to colonialism; this is particularly the case with the Fulas as, in Guinea, the Fulas were already conquerors (the Portuguese allied themselves with the Fulas in order to dominate Guinea at the beginning of the conquest). Thus, the chiefs (and their authority as chiefs) are very closely tied to the Portuguese authorities. The artisans are extremely dependent on the chiefs; they live off what they make for the chiefs, who are the only ones who can acquire their products, so there are some artisans who are simply content to follow the chiefs; then there are other people who try to break away and are well-disposed towards opposition to Portuguese colonialism. The main point about the Dyulas is that their permanent preoccupation is to protect their own personal interests; at least in Guinea, the Dyulas are not settled in any one place, they are itinerant traders without any real roots anywhere and their fundamental aim is to make bigger and bigger profits. It is precisely the fact that they are almost permanently on the move that provided us with a most valuable element in the struggle. It goes without saying that there are some who have not supported our struggle and there are some who have been used as agents against us by the Portuguese, but there are some whom we have been able to use to mobilize people, at least as far as spreading the initial ideas of the struggle was concerned—all we had to do was give them some reward, as they usually would not do anything without being paid.

Obviously, the group with the greatest interest in the struggle is the peasantry, given the nature of the various different societies in Guinea (feudal, semi-feudal, etc.) and the various degrees of exploitation to which they are subjected; but the question is not simply one of objective interest.

Given the general context of our traditions, or rather the superstructure created by the economic conditions in Guinea, the Fula peasants have a strong tendency to follow their chiefs. Thorough and intensive work was therefore needed to mobilize them. Among the Balantes and the groups without any defined form of state organization, the first point to note is that there are still a lot of remnants of animist traditions even among the Muslims in Guinea. The part of the population that follows Islam is not really Islamic but rather Islamized. They are animists who have adopted some Muslim practices, but are still thoroughly impregnated with animist conceptions. What is more, these groups without any defined organization put up much more resistance against the Portuguese than the others, and they have maintained intact their tradition of resistance to colonial penetration. This is the group that we found most ready to accept the idea of national liberation.

Here I should like to broach one key problem, which is of enormous importance for us, as we are a country of peasants, and that is the problem of whether or not the peasantry represents the main revolutionary force. I shall confine myself to my own country, Guinea, where it must be said at once that the peasantry is not a revolutionary force—which may seem strange, particularly as we have based the whole of our armed liberation struggle on the peasantry. A distinction must be drawn between a physical force and a revolutionary force. Physically, the peasantry is a great force in Guinea; it is almost the whole of the population; it controls the nation's wealth; it is the peasantry who produces. But we know from experience what trouble we had convincing the peasantry to fight. This is a problem I shall come back to later; here I should just like to refer to what the previous speaker said about China. The conditions of the peasantry in China were very different; the peasantry had a history of revolt, but this was not the case in Guinea, and so it was not possible for our party militants and propaganda workers to find the same kind of welcome among the peasantry in Guinea for the idea of national liberation as the idea found in China. All the same, in certain parts of the country and among certain groups, we found a very warm welcome, even right at the start. In other groups and in other areas, all this had to be won.

Then there are the positions vis-à-vis the struggle of the various groups in the towns to be considered. The Europeans are, in general, hostile to the idea of national liberation; they are the human instruments of the colonial state in our country, and they therefore reject a priori any idea of national liberation there. It has to be said that the Europeans most bitterly opposed to the idea of national liberation are the workers, while we have sometimes found considerable sympathy for our struggle among certain members of the European petite bourgeoisie.

As for the Africans, the petite bourgeoisie can be divided into three subgroups as regards the national liberation struggle. First, there is the petite bourgeoisie, which is heavily committed, and compromised with colonialism; this includes most of the higher officials and some members of the liberal professions. Second, there is the group that we perhaps incorrectly call the revolutionary petite bourgeoisie; this is the part of the petite bourgeoisie that is nationalist and that was the source of the idea of the national liberation struggle in Guinea. In between lies the part of the petite bourgeoisie that has never been able to make up its mind between the national liberation struggle and the Portuguese. Next come the wage-earners, whom you can compare roughly with the proletariat in European societies, although they are not exactly the same thing; here, too, there is a majority committed to the struggle, but again, many members of this group were not easy to mobilize—wage-earners who had an extremely petit bourgeois mentality and whose only aim was to defend the little they had already acquired.

Next come the déclassés. The really déclassé people, the permanent layabouts, the prostitutes, and so on have been a great help to the Portuguese police in giving them information; this group has been outrightly against our struggle, perhaps unconsciously so, but nonetheless against our struggle. On the other hand, the particular group I mentioned earlier, for which we have not yet found any precise classification (the group of mainly young people recently arrived from the rural areas with contacts in both the urban and the rural areas), gradually comes to make a comparison between the standard of living of their own families and that of the Portuguese; they begin to understand the sacrifices being borne by the Africans. They have proved extremely dynamic in the struggle. Many of these people joined the struggle right from the beginning, and it is among this group that we found many of the cadres that we have since trained.

The importance of this urban experience lies in the fact that it allows comparison; this is the key stimulant required for the awakening of consciousness. It is interesting to note that Algerian nationalism largely sprang up among the émigré workers in France. As far as Guinea is concerned, the idea of the national liberation struggle was born not abroad but in our own country, in a milieu where people were subjected to close and incessant exploitation. Many people say that it is the peasants who carry the burden of exploitation; this may be true, but so far as the struggle is concerned, it must be realized that it is not the degree of suffering and hardship involved as such that matters. Even extreme suffering in itself does not necessarily produce the *prise de conscience* required for the national liberation struggle. In Guinea the peasants are subjected to a kind of exploitation equivalent to slavery; but even if you try and explain to them that they are being exploited and robbed, it is difficult to convince them by means of an unexperienced explanation of a techno-economic kind that they are the most exploited people; whereas it is easier to convince the workers and the people employed in the towns who earn, say, ten escudos a day for a job at which a European earns between thirty and fifty that they are being subjected to massive exploitation and injustice, because they can see. To take my own case as a member of the petit bourgeois group that launched the struggle in Guinea, I was an agronomist working under a European whom everybody knew was one of the biggest idiots in Guinea. I could have taught him his job with my eyes shut but he was the boss; this is something which counts a lot, this is the confrontation which really matters. This is of major importance when considering where the initial idea of the struggle came from.

Another major task was to examine the material interests and the aspirations of each group after the liberation, as well as its revolutionary capacities. As I have already said, we do not consider that the peasantry in Guinea has a revolutionary capacity. First of all, we had to make an analysis of all these groups and of the contradictions between them and within them so as to be able to locate them all vis-à-vis the struggle and the revolution.

The first point is to decide what is the major contradiction at the moment when the struggle begins. For us, the main contradiction was that between, on the one hand, the Portuguese and international bourgeoisie that was exploiting our people, and, on the other hand, the interests of our people. There are also major contradictions within the country itself, that is, in the internal life of our country. It is our opinion that, if we get rid of colonialism in Guinea, the main contradiction remaining, the one that will then become the principal contradiction, is that between the ruling classes, the semi-feudal groups, and the members of the groups without any defined form of organization. The first thing to note is that the conquest carried out first by the Mandingues and then by the Fulas was a struggle between two opposite poles, which was blocked by the very strong structure of the animist groups.

There are other contradictions, such as that between the various feudal groups and that between the upper group and the lower. All this is extremely important for the future, and even while the struggle is still going on, we must begin to exploit the contradiction between the Fula people and their chiefs, who are very close to the Portuguese. There is a further contradiction, particularly among the animists, between the collective ownership of the land and the private ownership of the means of production in agriculture. I am not trying to stretch alien concepts here; this is an observation that can be made on the spot: the land belongs to the village, but what is produced belongs to whoever produces it—usually the family or the head of the family.

There are other contradictions that we consider secondary. You may be surprised to know that we consider the contradictions between the tribes a secondary one; we could discuss this at length, but we consider that there are many more contradictions between what you might call the economic tribes in the capitalist countries than there are between the ethnic tribes in Guinea. Our struggle for national liberation and the work done by our Party have shown that this contradiction is really not so important; the Portuguese counted on it a lot, but as soon as we organized the liberation struggle properly, the contradiction between the tribes proved to be a feeble, secondary contradiction. This does not mean that we do not need to pay attention to this contradiction; we reject both the positions that are to be found in Africa: One that says there are no tribes, we are all the same, we are all one people in one terrible unity, our party comprises everybody; the other saying tribes exist, we must base parties on tribes. Our position lies between the two, but at the same time we are fully conscious that this is a problem that must constantly be kept in mind; structural, organizational, and other measures must be taken to ensure that this contradiction does not explode and become a more important contradiction.

As for contradictions between the urban and rural areas, I would say that there is no conflict between the towns and the countryside, not least because we are only town dwellers who have just moved from the country; everybody in the towns in Guinea has close relatives in the country, and all town dwellers still engage in some peasant activity (growing crops, etc.). All the same, there is a potential contradiction between the towns and the countryside that colonialism tries to aggravate.

That, in brief, is the analysis we have made of the situation. This has led us to the following conclusion: we must try to unite everybody in the national liberation struggle against the Portuguese colonialists. This is where our main contradiction lies, but it is also imperative to organize things so that we always have an instrument available that can solve all the other contradictions. This is what convinced us of the absolute necessity of creating a party during the national liberation struggle. There are some people who interpret our Party as a front; perhaps our Party is a front at the moment, but within the framework of the front there is our Party that is directing the front, and there are no other parties in the front. For the circumstances of the struggle, we maintain a general aspect, but within the framework of the struggle, we know what our Party is, we know where the Party finishes and where the people who just rallied for the liberation struggle begin.

When we had made our analysis, there were still many theoretical and practical problems left in front of us. We had some knowledge of other experiences, and we knew that a struggle of the kind we hoped to lead—and win—had to be led by the working class; we looked for the working class in Guinea and did not find it. Other examples showed us that things were begun by some revolutionary intellectuals. What then were we to do? We were just a group of petit bourgeois who were driven by the reality of life in Guinea, by the sufferings we had to endure, and also by the influence events in Africa and elsewhere had on us, in particular the experiences some of us acquired in Portugal and other countries in Europe, to try and do something.

And so, this little group began. We first thought of a general movement of national liberation, but this immediately proved unfeasible. We decided to extend our activity to the workers in the towns, and we had some success with this; we launched moves for higher wages, better working conditions, and so on. I do not want to go into details here, the only point I want to make is that we obviously did not have a proletariat. We quite clearly lacked revolutionary intellectuals, so we had to start searching, given that we—rightly—did not believe in the revolutionary capacity of the peasantry.

One important group in the towns were the dockworkers; another important group were the people working in the boats carrying merchandise, who mostly live in Bissau itself and travel up and down the rivers. These people proved highly conscious of their position and of their economic importance, and they took the initiative of launching strikes without any trade union leadership at all. We therefore decided to concentrate all our work on this group. This gave excellent results, and this group soon came to form a kind of nucleus that influenced the attitudes of other wage-earning groups in the towns—workers proper and drivers, who form two other important groups. Moreover, if I may put it this way, we thus found our little proletariat.

We also looked for intellectuals, but there were none, because the Portuguese did not educate people. In any case, what is an intellectual in our country? It could probably be someone who knew the general situation very well, who had some knowledge, not profound theoretical knowledge, but concrete knowledge of the country itself and of its life, as well as of our enemy. We, the people I have talked about, the engineers, doctors, bank clerks, and so on, joined together to form a group of *interlocuteurs valables*.

There was also this other group of people in the towns, which we have been unable to classify precisely, that was still closely connected to the rural areas and contained people who spoke almost all the languages that are used in Guinea. They knew all the customs of the rural areas, while at the same time possessing a solid knowledge of the European urban centers. They also had a certain degree of self-confidence; they knew how to read and write (which makes a person an intellectual in our country), and so we concentrated our work on these people and immediately started giving them some preparatory training.

We were faced with another difficult problem; we realized that we needed to have people with a mentality that could transcend the context of the national liberation struggle, and so we prepared a number of cadres from the group I have just mentioned, some from the people employed in commerce and other wage-earners, and even some peasants, so that they could acquire what you might call a working-class mentality. You may think this is absurd—in any case, it is very difficult; in order for there to be a working-class mentality the material conditions of the working class should exist, a working class should exist. In fact, we managed to inculcate these ideas into a large number of people—the kind of ideas that there would be if there were a working class. We trained about one thousand cadres at our party school in Conakry, in fact for about two years this was about all we did outside the country. When these cadres returned to the rural areas, they inculcated a certain mentality into the peasants, and it is among these cadres that we have chosen the people who are now leading the struggle. We are not a Communist party or a Marxist-Leninist party, but the people now leading the peasants in the struggle in Guinea are mostly from the urban milieux and connected with the urban wage-earning group. When I hear that only the peasantry can lead the struggle, am I supposed to think we have made a mistake? All I can say is that, at the moment, our struggle is going well.

There are all sorts of other generalizations of a political nature, like this generalization about the peasantry, which keeps on cropping up. There are a number of key words and concepts, there is a certain conditioning in the reasoning of our European friends; for example, when someone thinks, "revolution," he thinks of the bourgeoisie falling, etc.; when someone thinks "party," he forgets many things. Yesterday a friend asked me a number of questions about our party and several times I had to say to him, "But it isn't a European party." The concept of a party and the creation of parties did not occur spontaneously in Europe; they resulted from a long process of class struggle. When we in Africa think of creating a party now, we find ourselves in very different conditions from those in which parties appeared as historico-social phenomena in Europe. This has a number of consequences, so when you think "party," "single party," etc., you must connect all these things up with the history and conditions of Africa.

A rigorous historical approach is similarly needed when examining another problem related to this—how can the underdeveloped countries evolve towards revolution, towards socialism? There is a preconception held by many people, even on the left, that imperialism made us enter history at the moment when it began its adventure in our countries. This preconception must be denounced; for somebody on the left, and for Marxists in particular, history obviously means the class struggle. Our opinion is exactly the contrary. We consider that when imperialism arrived in Guinea it made us leave history—our history. We agree that history in our country is the result of class struggle, but we have our own class struggles in our own country; the moment imperialism arrived and colonialism arrived, it made us leave our history and enter another history. Obviously, we agree that the class struggle has continued, but it has continued in a very different way; our whole people is struggling against the ruling class of the imperialist countries, and this gives a completely different aspect to the historical evolution of our country. Somebody has asked which class is the "agent" of history; here, a distinction must be drawn between colonial history and our history as human societies; as a dominated people, we only present an ensemble vis-à-vis the oppressor. Each of our peoples or groups of peoples has been subjected to different influences by the colonizers; when there is a developed national consciousness one may ask which social stratum is the agent of history, of colonial history; which is the stratum that will be able to take power into its hands when it emerges from colonial history? Our answer is that it is all the social strata, if the people who have carried out the national revolution (that is, the struggle against colonialism) have worked well, since unity of all the social strata is a prerequisite for the success of the national liberation struggle. As we see it, in colonial conditions no one stratum can succeed in the struggle for national liberation on its own, and therefore it is all the strata of society that are the agents of history. This brings us to what should be a void—but in fact it is not. What commands history in colonial conditions is not the class struggle. I do not mean that the class struggle in Guinea stopped completely during the colonial period; it continued, but in a muted way. In the colonial period it is the colonial state that commands history.

Our problem is to see who is capable of taking control of the state apparatus when the colonial power is destroyed. In Guinea the peasants cannot read or write, they have almost no relations with the colonial forces during the colonial period except for paying taxes, which is done indirectly. The working class hardly exists as a defined class, it is just an embryo. There is no economically viable bourgeoisie because imperialism prevented it being created. What there is is a stratum of people in the service of imperialism who have learned how to manipulate the apparatus of the state—the African petite bourgeoisie. This is the only stratum capable of controlling or even utilizing the instruments that the colonial state used against our people. So we come to the conclusion that, in colonial conditions, it is the petite bourgeoisie that is the inheritor of state power (though I wish we could be wrong). The moment national liberation comes and the petite bourgeoisie takes power, we enter, or rather return to history, and thus the internal contradictions break out again.

When this happens, and particularly as things are now, there will be powerful external contradictions conditioning the internal situation, and not just internal contradictions as before. What attitude can the petite bourgeoisie adopt? Obviously, people on the left will call for the revolution; the right will call for the "non-revolution," that is, a capitalist road or something like that. The petite bourgeoisie can either ally itself with imperialism and the reactionary strata in its own country to try and preserve itself as a petite bourgeoisie, or ally itself with the workers and peasants, who must themselves take power or control to make the revolution. We must be very clear exactly what we are asking the petite bourgeoisie to do. Are we asking it to commit suicide? Because if there is a revolution, then the petite bourgeoisie will have to abandon power to the workers and the peasants and cease to exist qua petite bourgeoisie. For a revolution to take place depends on the nature of the party (and its size), the character of the struggle that led up to liberation, whether there was an armed struggle, what the nature of this armed struggle was and how it developed, and, of course, on the nature of the state.

Here I would like to say something about the position of our friends on the left. If a petite bourgeoisie comes to power, they obviously demand of it that it carry out a revolution. But the important thing is whether they took the precaution of analyzing the position of the petite bourgeoisie during the struggle; did they examine its nature, see how it worked, see what instruments it used, and see whether this bourgeoisie committed itself with the left to carrying out a revolution, before the liberation? As you can see, it is the struggle in the underdeveloped countries that endows the petite bourgeoisie with a function; in the capitalist countries the petite bourgeoisie is only a stratum that serves. It does not determine the historical orientation of the country; it merely allies itself with one group or another. So that to hope that the petite bourgeoisie will just carry out a revolution when it comes to power in an underdeveloped country is to hope for a miracle, although it is true that it could do this.

This connects with the problem of the true nature of the national liberation struggle. In Guinea, as in other countries, the implantation of imperialism by force and the presence of the colonial system considerably altered the historical conditions and aroused a response—the national liberation struggle—which is generally considered a revolutionary trend; but this is something that I think needs further examination. I should like to formulate this question—is the national liberation movement something that has simply emerged from within our country, is it a result of the internal contradictions created by the presence of colonialism, or are there external factors that have determined it? And here we have some reservations; in fact, I would even go so far as to ask whether, given the advance of socialism in the world, the national liberation movement is not an imperialist initiative. Is the judicial institution that serves as a reference for the right of all peoples to struggle to free themselves a product of the peoples who are trying to liberate themselves? Was it created by the socialist countries who are our historical associates?

It is signed by the imperialist countries, it is the imperialist countries that have recognized the right of all peoples to national independence, so I ask myself whether we may not be considering as an initiative of our people what is in fact an initiative of the enemy? Even Portugal, which is using napalm bombs against our people in Guinea, signed the declaration of the right of all peoples to independence. One may well ask oneself why they were so mad as to do something that goes against their own interests—and whether or not it was partly forced on them, the real point is that they signed it. This is where we think there is something wrong with the simple interpretation of the national liberation movement as a revolutionary trend. The objective of the imperialist countries was to prevent the enlargement of the socialist camp, to liberate the reactionary forces in our countries that were being stifled by colonialism, and to enable these forces to ally themselves with the international bourgeoisie. The fundamental objective was to create a bourgeoisie where one did not exist, in order specifically to strengthen the imperialist and the capitalist camps. This rise of the bourgeoisie in the new countries, far from being at all surprising, should be considered absolutely normal, it is something that has to be faced by all those struggling against imperialism. We are therefore faced with the problem of deciding whether to engage in an out-and-out struggle against the bourgeoisie right from the start or whether to try and make an alliance with the national bourgeoisie, to try to deepen the absolutely necessary contradiction between the national bourgeoisie and the international bourgeoisie, which has promoted the national bourgeoisie to the position it holds.

To return to the question of the nature of the petite bourgeoisie and the role it can play after the liberation, I should like to put a question to you. What would you have thought if Fidel Castro had come to terms with the Americans? Is this possible or not? Is it possible or impossible that the Cuban petite bourgeoisie, which set the Cuban people marching towards revolution, might have come to terms with the Americans? I think this helps to clarify the character of the revolutionary petite bourgeoisie. If I may put it this way, I think one thing that can be said is this: the revolutionary petite bourgeoisie is honest; that is, in spite of all the hostile conditions, it remains identified with the fundamental interests of the popular masses. To do this, it may have to commit suicide, but it will not lose; by sacrificing itself it can reincarnate itself, but in the condition of workers or peasants. In speaking of honesty, I am not trying to establish moral criteria for judging the role of the petite bourgeoisie when it is in power; what I mean by honesty, in a political context, is total commitment and total identification with the toiling masses.

Again, the role of the petite bourgeoisie ties up with the possible social and political transformations that can be effected after liberation. We have heard a great deal about the state of national democracy, but although we have made every effort, we have thus far been unable to understand what this means; even so, we should like to know what it is all about, as we want to know what we are going to do when we have driven out the Portuguese. Likewise, we have to face the question whether or not socialism can be established immediately after the liberation. This depends on the instruments used to effect the transition to socialism; the essential factor is the nature of the state, bearing in mind that after the liberation there will be people controlling the police, the prisons, the army, and so on, and a great deal depends on who they are and what they try to do with these instruments. Thus, we return again to the problem of which class is the agent of history and who are the inheritors of the colonial state in our specific conditions.

I mentioned briefly earlier the question of the attitude of the European left towards the underdeveloped countries, in which there is a good deal of criticism and a good deal of optimism. The criticism reminds me of a story about some lions. There is a group of lions who are shown a picture of a lion lying on the ground and a man holding a gun with his foot on the lion (as everybody knows, the lion is proud of being king of the jungle); one of the lions looks at the picture and says, "If only we lions could paint." If one of the leaders of one of the new African countries could take time off from the terrible problems in his own country and become a critic of the European left and say all he had to say about the retreat of the revolution in Europe, of a certain apathy in some European countries, and of the false hopes that we have all had in certain European groups . . . .

What really interests us here is neocolonialism. After the Second World War, imperialism entered on a new phase—on the one hand, it worked out the new policy of aid, that is, granted independence to the occupied countries plus "aid" and, on the other hand, concentrated on preferential investment in the European countries; this was, above all, an attempt at rationalizing imperialism. Even if it has not yet provoked reactions of a nationalist kind in the European countries, we are convinced that it will soon do so. As we see it, neocolonialism (which we may call rationalized imperialism) is more a defeat for the international working class than for the colonized peoples. Neocolonialism is at work on two fronts—in Europe as well as in the underdeveloped countries. Its current framework in the underdeveloped countries is the policy of aid, and one of the essential aims of this policy is to create a false bourgeoisie to put a brake on the revolution and to enlarge the possibilities of the petite bourgeoisie as a neutralizer of the revolution; at the same time, it invests capital in France, Italy, Belgium, England, and so on. In our opinion, the aim of this is to stimulate the growth of a workers' aristocracy, to enlarge the field of action of the petite bourgeoisie so as to block the revolution. In our opinion, it is under this aspect that neocolonialism and the relations between the international working-class movement and our movements must be analyzed.

If there have ever been any doubts about the close relations between our struggle and the struggle of the international working-class movement, neocolonialism has proved that there need not be any. Obviously, I don't think it is possible to forge closer relations between the peasantry in Guinea and the working-class movement in Europe; what we must do first is try and forge closer links between the peasant movement and the wage-earners' movement in our own country. The example of Latin America gives you a good idea of the limits on closer relations; in Latin America you have an old neocolonial situation and a chance to see clearly the relations between the North American proletariat and the Latin American masses. Other examples could be found nearer home.

There is, however, another aspect I should like to raise, and that is that the European left has an intellectual responsibility to study the concrete conditions in our country and help us in this way, as we have very little documentation, very few intellectuals, very little chance to do this kind of work ourselves, and yet it is of key importance; this is a major contribution you can make. Another thing you can do is to support the really revolutionary national liberation movements by all possible means. You must analyze and study these movements and combat in Europe, by all possible means, everything that can be used to further the repression against our peoples. I refer especially to the sale of arms. I should like to say to our Italian friends that we have captured a lot of Italian arms from the Portuguese, not to mention French arms, of course. Moreover, you must unmask courageously all the national liberation movements that are under the thumb of imperialism. People whisper that so-and-so is an American agent, but nobody in the European left has taken a violent and open attitude against these people; it is we ourselves who have to try and denounce these people, who are sometimes even those accepted by the rest of Africa, and this creates a lot of trouble for us.

I think that the left and the international working-class movement should confront those states that claim to be socialist with their responsibilities; this does not, of course, mean cutting off all their possibilities of action, but it does mean denouncing all those states that are neocolonialist.

To end up with, I should just like to make one last point about solidarity between the international working-class movement and our national liberation struggle. There are two alternatives: Either we admit that there really is a struggle against imperialism that interests everybody, or we deny it. If, as would seem from all the evidence, imperialism exists and is trying simultaneously to dominate the working class in all the advanced countries and smother the national liberation movements in all the underdeveloped countries, then there is only one enemy against whom we are fighting. If we are fighting together, then I think the main aspect of our solidarity is extremely simple: It is to fight—I don't think there is any need to discuss this very much. We are struggling in Guinea with guns in our hands, you must struggle in your countries, as well—I don't say with guns in your hands, I'm not going to tell you how to struggle, that's your business; but you must find the best means and the best forms of fighting against our common enemy—this is the best form of solidarity.

There are, of course, other secondary forms of solidarity—publishing material, sending medicine, etc.; I can guarantee you that, if tomorrow, we make a breakthrough and you are engaged in an armed struggle against imperialism in Europe, we will send you some medicine, too.

— 6 —

Identity and Dignity in the Context of the National Liberation Struggle

On October 15, 1972, Amilcar Cabral received an honorary doctorate degree at Lincoln University, Pennsylvania. This was his address on that occasion.

Introduction

The people's struggle for national liberation and independence from imperialist rule has become a driving force of progress for humanity and undoubtedly constitutes one of the essential characteristics of contemporary history.

An objective analysis of imperialism, insofar as it is a fact or a "natural" historical phenomenon, indeed "necessary" in the context of the type of economic political evolution of an important part of humanity, reveals that imperialist rule, with all its train of wretchedness, of pillage, of crime, and of destruction of human and cultural values, was not just a negative reality. The vast accumulation of capital in half a dozen countries of the Northern Hemisphere, which was the result of piracy, of the confiscation of the property of other peoples, and of the ruthless exploitation of the work of these peoples, will not only lead to the monopolization of colonies, but to the division of the world, and more imperialist rule.

In the rich countries, imperialist capital, constantly seeking to enlarge itself, increased the creative capacity of man and brought about a total transformation of the means of production thanks to the rapid progress of science, of techniques, and of technology. This accentuated the pooling of labor and brought about the ascension of huge areas of population. In the colonized countries where colonization, on the whole, blocked the historical process of the development of the subjected peoples or else eliminated them radically or progressively, imperialist capital imposed new types of relationships on indigenous society, the structure of which became more complex. And it stirred up, fomented, poisoned, or resolved contradictions and social conflicts; it introduced, together with money and the development of internal and external markets, new elements in the economy; it brought about the birth of new nations from human groups or from peoples who were at different stages of historical development.

It is not to defend imperialist domination to recognize that it gave new nations to the world, the dimensions of which it reduced, and that it revealed new stages of development in human societies and, in spite of or because of the prejudices, the discrimination, and the crimes that it occasioned, it contributed to a deeper knowledge of humanity as a moving whole, as a unity in the complex diversity of the characteristics of its development.

Imperialist rule on many continents favored a multilateral and progressive (sometimes abrupt) confrontation not only between different men but also between different societies. The practice of imperialist rule—its affirmation or its negation—demanded (and still demands) a more or less accurate knowledge of the society it rules and of the historical reality (both economic, social, and cultural) in the middle of which it exists. This knowledge is necessarily exposed in terms of comparison with the dominating subject and with its own historical reality. Such a knowledge is a vital necessity in the practice of imperialist rule, which results in the confrontation, mostly violent, between two identities that are totally dissimilar in their historical elements and contradictory in their different functions. The search for such a knowledge contributed to a general enrichment of human and social knowledge, in spite of the fact that it was one-sided, subjective, and very often unjust.

In fact, man has never shown as much interest in knowing other men and other societies as during this century of imperialist domination. An unprecedented mass of information, of hypotheses and theories, has been built up, notably in the fields of history, ethnology, ethnography, sociology, and culture concerning people or groups brought under imperialist domination. The concepts of race, caste, ethnicity, tribe, nation, culture, identity, dignity, and many others, have become the object of increasing attention from those who study men and the societies described as "primitive" or "evolving." More recently, with the rise of liberation movements, the need has arisen to analyze the character of these societies in the light of the struggle they are waging, and to decide the factors that launch or hold back this struggle. The researchers are generally agreed that, in this context, culture shows special significance. So one can argue that any attempt to clarify the true role of culture in the development of the (pre-independence) liberation movement can make a useful contribution to the broad struggle of the people against imperialist domination.

In this short lecture, we consider particularly the problems of the "return to the source," and of identity and dignity in the context of the national liberation movement.

Part 1

The fact that independence movements are generally marked, even in their early stages, by an upsurge of cultural activity, has led to the view that such movements are preceded by a "cultural renaissance" of the subject people. Some go as far as to suggest that culture is one means of collecting together a group, even a weapon in the struggle for independence.

From the experience of our own struggle, and one might say that of the whole of Africa, we consider that there is a too limited, even a mistaken, idea of the vital role of culture in the development of the liberation movement. In our view, this arises from a fake generalization of a phenomenon that is real but limited, that is at a particular level in the vertical structure of colonized societies—at the level of the elite or the colonial diasporas. This generalization is unaware of or ignores the vital element of the problem: the indestructible character of the cultural resistance of the masses of the people when confronted with foreign domination.

Certainly, imperialist domination calls for cultural oppression and attempts either directly or indirectly to do away with the most important elements of the culture of the subject people. But the people are only able to create and develop the liberation movement because they keep their culture alive despite continual and organized repression of their cultural life and because they continue to resist culturally, even when their politico-military resistance is destroyed. And it is cultural resistance that, at a given moment, can take on new forms, that is, political, economic, armed to fight foreign domination.

With certain exceptions, the period of colonization was not long enough, at least in Africa, for there to be a significant degree of destruction or damage of the most important facets of the culture and traditions of the subject people. Colonial experience of imperialist domination in Africa (genocide, racial segregation, and apartheid excepted) shows that the only so-called positive solution that the colonial power put forward to repudiate the subject people's cultural resistance was "assimilation." But the complete failure of the policy of "progressive assimilation" of native populations is the living proof, both of the falsehood of this theory and of the capacity of the subject people to resist. As far as the Portuguese colonies are concerned, the maximum number of people assimilated was 0.3 percent of the total population (in Guinea), and this was after five hundred years of civilizing influence and half a century of "colonial peace." On the other hand, even in the settlements where the overwhelming majority of the population is indigenous peoples, the area occupied by the colonial power and especially the area of cultural influence is usually restricted to coastal strips and to a few limited parts in the interior. Outside the boundaries of the capital and other urban centers, the influence of the colonial power's culture is almost nil. It only leaves its mark at the very top of the colonial social pyramid—which created colonialism itself—and particularly, it influences what one might call the "indigenous lower-middle class" and a very small number of workers in urban areas.

It can thus be seen that the masses in the rural areas, like a large section of the urban population, say, in all, over 99 percent of the indigenous population is untouched or almost untouched by the culture of the colonial power. This situation is partly the result of the necessarily obscurantist character of the imperialist domination, which, while it despises and suppresses indigenous culture, takes no interest in promoting culture for the masses who are their pool for forced labor and the main object of exploitation. It is also the result of the effectiveness of cultural resistance of the people, who, when they are subjected to political domination and economic exploitation, find that their own culture acts as a bulwark in preserving their identity. Where the indigenous society has a vertical structure, this defense of their cultural heritage is further strengthened by the colonial power's interest in protecting and backing the cultural influence of the ruling classes, their allies.

The above argument implies that, generally speaking, there is not any marked destruction or damage to culture or tradition, neither for the masses in the subject country, nor for the indigenous ruling classes (traditional chief, noble families, religious authorities). Repressed, persecuted, humiliated, betrayed by certain social groups that have compromised with the foreign power, culture takes refuge in the villages, in the forests, and in the spirit of the victims of domination. Culture survives all these challenges and, through the struggle for liberation, blossoms forth again. Thus, the question of a "return to the source" or of a "cultural renaissance" does not arise and could not arise for the masses of these people, for it is they who are the repository of the culture and at the same time the only social sector who can preserve and build it up and make history.

Thus, in Africa at least, for a true idea of the real role that culture plays in the development of the liberation movement, a distinction must be made between the situation of the masses, who preserve their culture, and that of the social groups who are assimilated or partially so, who are cut off and culturally alienated. Even though the indigenous colonial elite who emerged during the process of colonization still continue to pass on some element of indigenous culture, they live both materially and spiritually according to the foreign colonial culture. They seek to identify themselves increasingly with this culture, both in their social behaviors and even in their appreciation of its values.

In the course of two or three generations of colonization, a social class arises made up of civil servants, people who are employed in various branches of the economy, especially commerce, professional people, and a few urban and agricultural landowners. This indigenous petite bourgeoisie, which emerged out of foreign domination and is indispensable to the system of colonial exploitation, stands midway between the masses of the working class in town and country and the small number of local representatives of the foreign ruling class. Although they may have quite strong links with the masses and with the traditional chiefs, generally speaking, they aspire to a way of life that is similar if not identical with that of the foreign minority. At the same time, while they restrict their dealings with the masses, they try to become integrated into this minority, often at the cost of family or ethnic ties and always at great personal cost. Yet despite the apparent exceptions, they do not succeed in getting past the barriers thrown up by the system. They are prisoners of the cultural and social contradictions of their lives. They cannot escape from their role as a marginal class, or a "marginalized" class.

The marginal character or the "marginality" of this class, both in its own country and in the diasporas established in the territory of the colonial power, is responsible for the sociocultural conflicts of the colonial elite or the indigenous petite bourgeoisie, played out very much according to their material circumstances and level of acculturation, but always at the individual level, never collectively.

It is within the framework of this daily drama, against the backcloth of the usually violent confrontation between the mass of the people and the ruling colonial class, that a feeling of bitterness or a *frustration complex* is bred and develops among the indigenous petite bourgeoisie. At the same time, they are becoming more and more conscious of a compelling need to question their marginal status, and to rediscover an identity.

Thus, they turn to the people around them, the people at the other extreme of the sociocultural conflict—the native masses. For this reason arises the problem of a "return to the source," which seems to be even more pressing, the greater is the isolation of the petite bourgeoisie (or native elites) and their acute feelings of frustration, as in the case of African diasporas living in the colonial or racist metropolis. It comes as no surprise that the theories or "movements" such as Pan-Africanism or Negritude (two pertinent expressions arising mainly from the assumption that all Black Africans have a cultural identity) were propounded outside Black Africa. More recently, the Black Americans' claim to an African identity is another proof, possibly rather a desperate one, of the need for a "return to the source," although, clearly, it is influenced by a new situation: the fact that the great majority of African people are now independent.

But the "return to the source" is not and cannot in itself be an act of struggle against foreign domination (colonialist and racist), and it no longer necessarily means a return to traditions. It is the denial, by the petite bourgeoisie, of the pretended supremacy of the culture of the dominant power over that of the dominated people with which it must identify itself. The "return to the source" is therefore not a voluntary step, but the only possible reply to the demand of concrete need, historically determined, and enforced by the inescapable contradiction between the colonized society and the colonial power, the mass of the people exploited and the foreign exploitive class, a contradiction in the light of which each social stratum or indigenous class must define its position.

When the "return to the source" goes beyond the individual and is expressed through "groups" or "movements," the contradiction is transformed into struggle (secret or overt) and is a prelude to the pre-independence movement or to the struggle for liberation from the foreign yoke. So the "return to the source" is of no historical importance unless it brings not only real involvement in the struggle for independence, but also complete and absolute identification with the hopes of the mass of the people, who contest not only the foreign culture but also the foreign domination as a whole. Otherwise, the "return to the source" is nothing more than an attempt to find short-term benefits—knowingly or unknowingly a kind of political opportunism.

One must point out that the "return to the source," apparent or real, does not develop at one time and in the same way in the heart of the indigenous petite bourgeoisie. It is a slow process, broken up and uneven, whose development depends on the degree of acculturation of each individual, of the material circumstances of his life, on the forming of his ideas and on his experience as a social being. This unevenness is the basis of the split of the indigenous petite bourgeoisie into three groups when confronted with the liberation movement: a) a minority, which, even if it wants to see an end to foreign domination, clings to the dominant colonialist class and openly oppose the movement to protect its social position; b) a majority of people who are hesitant and indecisive;

c) another minority of people who share in the building and leadership of the liberation movement.

But the latter group, which plays a decisive role in the development of the pre-independence movement, does not truly identify with the mass of the people (with their culture and hopes) except through struggle, the scale of this identification depending on the kind or methods of struggle, on the ideological basis of the movement, and on the level of moral and political awareness of each individual.

Part II

Identification of a section of the indigenous petite bourgeoisie with the mass of the people has an essential prerequisite: that, in the face of destructive action by imperialist domination, the masses retain their identity, separate and distinct from that of the colonial power. It is worthwhile, therefore, to decide in what circumstances this retention is possible; why, when, and at what levels of the dominated society is raised the problem of the loss or absence of identity; and in consequence, it becomes necessary to assert or reassert in the framework of the pre-independence movement a separate and distinct identity from that of the colonial power.

The identity of an individual or a particular group of people is a bio-sociological factor outside the will of that individual or group, but is meaningful only when it is expressed in relation to other individuals or other groups. The dialectical character of identity lies in the fact that an individual (or a group) is only similar to certain individuals (or groups) if it is also different from other individuals (or groups).

The definition of an identity, individual or collective, is at the same time the affirmation and denial of a certain number of characteristics that define the individuals or groups, through *historical* (biological and sociological) factors at a moment of their development. In fact, identity is not a constant, precisely because the biological and sociological factors that define it are in constant change. Biologically and sociologically, there are no two beings (individual or collective) completely the same or completely different, for it is always possible to find in them common or distinguishing characteristics. Therefore, the identity of a being is always a relative quality, even circumstantial, for defining it demands a selection, more or less rigid and strict, of the biological and sociological characteristics of the being in question. One must point out that, in the fundamental binomial in the definition of identity, the sociological factors are more determining than the biological. In fact, if it is correct that the biological element (inherited genetic patrimony) is the inescapable physical basis of the existence and continuing growth of identity, it is no less correct that the sociological element is the factor that gives it objective substance by giving content and form and allowing confrontation and comparison between individuals and between groups. To make a total definition of identity, the inclusion of the biological element is indispensable, but does not imply a sociological similarity, whereas two beings who are sociologically exactly the same must necessarily have similar biological identities.

This shows, on the one hand, the supremacy of the social over the individual condition, for society (human, for example) is a higher form of life. It shows, on the other hand, the need not to confuse the original identity, of which the biological element is the main determinant, and the actual identity of which the main determinant is the sociological element. Clearly, the identity of which one must take account at a given moment of the growth of a being (individual or collective) is the actual identity, and awareness of that being reached only on the basis of his original identity is incomplete, partial, and false, for it leaves out or does not comprehend the decisive influence of social conditions on the content and form of identity.

In the formation and development of individual or collective identity, the social condition is an objective agent, arising from economic, political, social, and cultural aspects that are characteristic of the growth and history of the society in question. If one argues that the economic aspect is fundamental, one can assert that identity is, in a certain sense, the expression of an economic reality. This reality, whatever the geographical context and the path of development of the society, is defined by the level of productive forces (the relationship between man and nature) and by the means of production (the relations between men and between classes within this society). But if one accepts that culture is a dynamic synthesis of the material and spiritual condition of the society, and expresses relationship both between man and nature and between the different classes within a society, one can assert that identity is at the individual and collective level and beyond the economic condition, the expression of culture. This is why to attribute, recognize, or declare the identity of an individual or group is above all to place that individual or group in the framework of a culture. Now, as we all know, the main prop of culture in any society is the social structure. One can, therefore, draw the conclusion that the possibility of a movement group keeping (or losing) its identity in the face of foreign domination depends on the extent of the destruction of its social structure under the stresses of that domination.

As for the effects of imperialist domination on the social structure of the dominated people, one must look here at the case of classic colonialism against which the pre-independence movement is contending. In that case, whatever the stage of historical development of the dominated society, the social structure can be subjected to the following experiences: a) total destruction, mixed with immediate or gradual liquidation of the indigenous people and replacement by a foreign people; b) partial destruction, with the settling of a more or less numerous foreign population; c) ostensible preservation, brought about by the restriction of the indigenous people in geographical areas or special reserves, usually without means of living, and the massive influx of a foreign population.

The fundamentally horizontal character of the social structure of African people, due to the profusion of ethnic groups, means that the cultural resistance and degree of retention of identity are not uniform. So, even where ethnic groups have broadly succeeded in keeping their identity, we observe that the most resistant groups are those that have had the most violent battles with the colonial power during the period of effective occupation [in our country: Mandjaques, Pepels, Oincas, Balantes, Beafadas] or those who, because of their geographical location, have had least contact with the foreign presence [Pajadincas and other minorities in the interior]. One must point out that the attitude of the colonial power towards the ethnic groups creates an insoluble contradiction.

On the one hand, it must divide or keep divisions in order to rule and, for that reason, favors separation if not conflict between ethnic groups; on the other hand, to try to keep the permanency of its domination, it needs to destroy the social structure, culture, and, by implication, identity of these groups. Moreover, it must protect the ruling class of those groups that (for example, the Fula tribe or nation in our country) have given it decisive support during the colonial conquest—a policy that favors the preservation of the identity of these groups.

As has already been said, there are not usually important changes in respect of culture in the upright shape of the indigenous social pyramids (groups or societies with a state). Each level or class keeps its identity, linked with that of the group but separate from that of other social classes. Conversely, in the urban centers, as in some of the interior regions of the country where the cultural influence of the colonial power is felt, the problem of identity is more complicated. While the bottom and the top of the social pyramid (that is, the mass of the working class drawn from different ethnic groups and the foreign dominant class) keep their identities, the middle level of this pyramid (the indigenous petite bourgeoisie), culturally uprooted, alienated, or more or less assimilated, engages in a sociological battle in search of its identity. One must also point out that, though united by a new identity—granted by the colonial power—the foreign dominant class cannot free itself from the contradictions of its own society, which it brings to the colonized country.

When, at the initiative of a minority of the indigenous petite bourgeoisie, allied with the indigenous masses, the pre-independence movement is launched, the masses have no need to assert or reassert their identity, which they have never confused nor would have known how to confuse with that of the colonial power. This need is felt only by the indigenous petite bourgeoisie, which finds itself obliged to take up a position in the struggle that opposes the masses to the colonial power. However, the reassertion of identity distinct from that of the colonial power is not always achieved by all the petite bourgeoisie. It is only a minority who do this, while another minority asserts, often in a noisy manner, the identity of the foreign dominant class, while the silent majority is trapped in indecision.

Moreover, even when there is a reassertion of an identity distinct from that of the colonial power, therefore the same as that of the masses, it does not show itself in the same way everywhere. One part of the middle-class minority engaged in the pre-independence movement uses the foreign cultural norms, calling on literature and art, to express the discovery of its identity rather than to express the hopes and sufferings of the masses. And, precisely because it uses the language and speech of the minority colonial power, it only occasionally manages to influence the masses, generally illiterate and familiar with other forms of artistic expression. This does not, however, remove the value of the contribution for the development of the struggle made by this petite bourgeoise minority, for it can at the same time influence a sector of the uprooted, or those who are latecomers to its own class and an important sector of public opinion in the colonial metropolis, notably the class of intellectuals.

The other part of the lower middle class that, from the start, joins in the pre-independence movement, finds in its prompt share in the liberation struggle and in integration with the masses the best means of expression of identity distinct from that of the colonial power.

That is why identification with the masses and reassertion of identity can be temporary or definitive, apparent or real, in the light of the daily efforts and sacrifices demanded by the struggle itself. A struggle, which, while being the organized political expression of a *culture*, is also and necessarily a proof not only of *identity* but also of *dignity*.

In the course of the process of colonialist domination, the masses, whatever the characteristic of the social structure of the group to which they belong, do not stop resisting the colonial power. In a first phase—that of conquest, cynically called "pacification"—they resist, gun in hand, foreign occupation. In a second phase—that of the golden age of triumphant colonialism—they offer the foreign domination passive resistance, almost silent, but blazoned with many revolts, usually individual and once in a while collective. The revolt is particularly in the field of work and taxes, even in social contacts with the representatives, foreign or indigenous, of the colonial power. In a third phase—that of the liberation struggle—it is the masses who provide the main strength that employs political or armed resistance to challenge and to destroy foreign domination. Such a prolonged and varied resistance is possible only because, while keeping their culture and identity, the masses keep intact the sense of their individual and collective dignity, despite the worries, humiliations, and brutalities to which they are often subjected.

The assertion or reassertion by the indigenous petite bourgeoisie of an identity distinct from that of the colonial power does not and could not bring about restoration of a sense of dignity to that class alone. In this context, we see that the sense of dignity of the petite bourgeoisie class depends on the objective moral and social feeling of each individual, on his subjective attitude towards the two poles of the colonial conflict, between which he is forced to live out the daily drama of colonialization. This drama is the more shattering to the extent to which the petite bourgeoisie, in fulfilling its role, is made to live alongside both the foreign dominating class and the masses. On one side, the petite bourgeoisie is the victim of frequent if not daily humiliation by the foreigner, and, on the other side, it is aware of the injustice to which the masses are subjected and of their resistance and spirit of rebellion. Hence arises the apparent paradox of colonial domination; it is from within the indigenous petite bourgeoisie, a social class that grows from colonialism itself, that arise the first important steps towards mobilizing and organizing the masses for the struggle against the colonial power.

The struggle, in the face of all kinds of obstacles and in a variety of forms, reflects the awareness or grasp of a complete identity, generalizes and consolidates the sense of dignity, strengthened by the development of political awareness, and derives from the culture or cultures of the masses in revolt one of its principal strengths.

— 7 —

Connecting the Struggles: An Informal Talk with Black Americans

During his last visit to the United States, Cabral asked the Africa Information Service to organize a small informal meeting at which he could speak with representatives of different Black organizations. The A.I.S. contacted approximately thirty organizations, and on October 20, 1972, more than 120 people representing a wide range of Black groups in America crowded into a small room to meet with Amilcar Cabral. A number of the people present came to New York City specifically for this meeting. At the meeting, the vitality, warmth, and humor of Cabral the person became evident to those who had not met him before. Parts of the discussion have been edited (grammatically) to compensate for the fact that, although Cabral spoke many languages, English was not his most comfortable language.

I am bringing to you—our African brothers and sisters of the United States—the fraternal salutations of our people in assuring you we are very conscious that all in this life concerning you also concerns us. If we do not always pronounce words that clearly show this, it doesn't mean that we are not conscious of it. It is a reality, and considering that the world is being made smaller each day, all people are becoming conscious of this fact.

Naturally, if you ask me between brothers and comrades what I prefer—if we are brothers, it is not our fault or our responsibility. But if we are comrades, it is a political engagement. Naturally, we like our brothers, but in our conception, it is better to be a brother and a comrade. We like our brothers very much, but we think that if we are brothers, we have to realize the responsibility of this fact and take clear positions about our problems in order to see if, beyond this condition of brothers, we are also comrades. This is very important for us.

We try to understand your situation in this country. You can be sure that we realize the difficulties you face, the problems you have and your feelings, your revolts, and also your hopes. We think that our fighting for Africa against colonialism and imperialism is a proof of understanding your problem and also a contribution to the solution of your problems in this continent. Naturally, the inverse is also true. All the achievements towards the solution of your problems here are real contributions to our own struggle. And we are very encouraged in our struggle by the fact that each day more of the African people born in America become conscious of their responsibilities to the struggle in Africa.

Does that mean you have to all leave here and go fight in Africa? We do not believe so. That is not being realistic, in our opinion. History is a very strong chain. We have to accept the limits of history, but not the limits imposed by the societies where we are living. There is a difference. We think that all you can do here to develop your own conditions in the sense of progress, in the sense of history and in the sense of the total realization of your aspirations as human beings, is a contribution for us. It is also a contribution for you to never forget that you are Africans.

Does that mean that we are racists? No! We are not racists. We are fundamentally and deeply against any kind of racism. Even when people are subjected to racism, we are against racism from those who have been oppressed by it. In our opinion—not from dreaming but from a deep analysis of the real conditions of the existence of mankind and of the division of societies—racism is a result of certain circumstances. It is not eternal in any latitude in the world. It is the result of historical and economic conditions. And we cannot answer racism with racism. It is not possible. In our country, despite some racist manifestations by the Portuguese, we are not fighting against the Portuguese people or whites. We are fighting for the freedom of our people—to free our people and to allow them to be able to love any kind of human being. You cannot love if you are a slave. It is very difficult.

In combatting racism, we don't make progress if we combat the people themselves. We have to combat the causes of racism. If a bandit comes in my house and I have a gun, I cannot shoot the shadow of this bandit. I have to shoot the bandit. Many people lose energy and effort and make sacrifices combatting shadows. We have to combat the material reality that produces the shadow. If we cannot change the light that is one cause of the shadow, we can at least change the body. It is important to avoid confusion between the shadow and the body that projects the shadow. We are encouraged by the fact that, each day, more of our people, here and in Africa, realize this reality. This reinforces our confidence in our final victory.

The fact that you follow our struggle and are interested in our achievements is good for us. We base our struggle on the concrete realities of our country. We appreciate the experiences and achievements of other peoples and we study them. But revolution or national liberation struggle is like a dress that must be fit to each individual's body. Naturally, there are certain general or universal laws, even scientific laws, for any condition, but the liberation struggle has to be developed according to the specific conditions of each country. This is fundamental.

The specific conditions to be considered include: economic, cultural, social, political, and even geographic. The guerrilla manuals once told us that, without mountains, you cannot make guerrilla war. But in my country, there are no mountains, only the people. In the economic field, we committed an error. We began training our people to commit sabotage on the railroads. When they returned from their training, we remembered that there were no railroads in our country. The Portuguese built them in Mozambique and Angola but not in our country.

There are other conditions to consider as well. You must consider the type of society in which you are fighting. Is it divided along horizontal lines or vertical lines? Some people tell us our struggle is the same as that of the Vietnamese people. It is similar but it is not the same. The Vietnamese are a people who, hundreds of years ago, fought against foreign invaders as a nation. We are now forging our nation in the struggle. This is a big difference. It is difficult to imagine what a difference that makes. Vietnam is also a society with clear social structures, with classes well defined. There is no national bourgeoisie in our country. A miserable, small petite bourgeoisie, yes, but not a national bourgeoisie. These differences are very important.

Once I discussed politics with Eldridge Cleaver. He is a clever man, very intelligent. We agreed on many things, but we disagreed on one thing. He told me your condition is a colonial condition. In certain aspects, it seems to be, but it is not really a colonial condition. The colonial condition demands certain factors. One important factor is continuity of territories. There are others that you can see when you analyze. Many times we are confronted with phenomena that seem to be the same, but political activity demands that we be able to distinguish them. That is not to say that the aims are not the same. And that is not to say that even some of the means cannot be the same. However, we must deeply analyze each situation to avoid loss of time and energy doing things that we should not do and forgetting things that we have to do.

In our country we have been fighting for nearly ten years. If we consider the changes achieved in that time, principally in the relationship between men and women, it has been more than one hundred years. If we were only shooting bullets and shells, yes, ten years is too much. But we were not only doing this. We were forging a nation during these years. How long did it take the European nations to be formed—ten centuries from the Middle Ages to the Renaissance. (Here in the United States you are still forging a nation—it is not yet completed, in my opinion. Several things have contributed to the forming and changing of this country, such as the Vietnam War, unfortunately, at the expense of the Vietnamese people. But you know the details of change in this country more than myself.)

Ten years ago, we were Fula, Mandjak, Mandinka, Balante, Pepel, and others. Now we are a nation of Guineans. Tribal divisions were one reason the Portuguese thought it would not be possible for us to fight. During these ten years, we were making more and more changes, so that today we can see that there is a new man and a new woman, born with our new nation and because of our fight. This is because of our ability to fight as a nation.

Naturally, we are not defending the armed fight. Maybe I deceive people, but I am not a great defender of the armed fight. I am myself very conscious of the sacrifices demanded by the armed fight. It is a violence against even our own people. But it is not our invention—it is not our cool decision; it is the requirement of history. This is not the first fight in our country, and it is not Cabral who invented the struggle. We are following the example given by our grandfathers who fought against Portuguese domination fifty years ago. Today's fight is a continuation of the fight to defend our dignity, our right to have an identity—our own identity.

If it were possible to solve this problem without the armed fight—why not!?! But, while the armed fight demands sacrifices, it also has advantages. Like everything else in the world, it has two faces—one positive, the other negative—the problem is in the balance. For us now, it [the armed fight] is a good thing in our opinion, and our condition is a good thing because this armed fight helps us to accelerate the revolution of our people, to create a new situation that will facilitate our progress.

In these ten years, we liberated about three-fourths of the country, and we are effectively controlling two-thirds of our country. We have much work to do, but we have our state, we have a strong political organization, a developing administration, and we have created many services—always while facing the bombs of the Portuguese. That is to say, bombs used by the Portuguese, but made in the United States. In the military field, we realized good things during these ten years. We have our national army and our local militias. We have even been able to receive a number of visitors—journalists, filmmakers, scientists, teachers, writers, government representatives, and others. We also received a special mission of the United Nations last April that made a very good report about the situation in our country.

However, through this armed fight, we realized other things more important than the size of the liberated regions or the capacity of our fighters, such as the irreversible change in the attitudes of our men. We have more sacrifices to make and more difficulties to overcome, but our people are now accustomed to this, and know that, for freedom, we must pay a price. What can we consider better than freedom? It is not possible—nothing compares with freedom. During the visit of the special mission of the UN to our country, one of the official observers, while on a long march, asked a small boy if he ever got tired. The boy answered, "I can't get tired—this is my country. Only the Portuguese soldiers get tired."

Now we can accelerate the process of the liberation of the rest of our country. Each day, we get more and better workers. Now we need more ammunition in order to give greater impact to our attacks against the Portuguese positions. Instead of attacking with eighty shells, we have to attack with eight hundred, if not two thousand, and we are preparing to do this. The situation is now better in the urban centers. We are dominating the urban centers in spite of the Portuguese occupation. Links with our underground organization in these centers are now very good, and we have decided to develop our action inside these centers.

We told this on the radio to the Portuguese. We told all of the people because the Portuguese cannot stop us. We told them before they would be afraid, and they are. They are even afraid of their shadows.

Another very positive aspect of our struggle is the political situation on the Cape Verde Islands. Some days ago, there were riots between our people and the police. This is a sign that great developments are coming within the framework of our fight on the Islands.

We have taken all measures demanded by the struggle, in the political as well as the military field. With the general election just completed in the liberated region, we are now creating our National Assembly. Naturally, we are not doing a National Assembly like the Congress you have here or the British Parliament. All these are very important steps in accelerating the end of the colonial war in my country and for its total liberation.

We have decided to formally proclaim our state, and we hope that our brothers and sisters here, our brothers and sisters in Africa, and our friends all over the world will take the necessary position of support for our new initiatives in this political field. In an armed fight like ours, all the political aspects have been stressed. They are stressed, naturally, when you approach the end. It is a dialectical process. In the beginning, the fight is political only, it is then followed by the transformation into the armed stage. Step by step, the political aspect returns, but at a different level, the level of the solution.

I am not going to develop these things further; I think it is better if you ask questions. We are very happy to be with you, our brothers and sisters. I tell you frankly, although it might hurt my visit to the United Nations: Each day, I feel myself more identified with you. I am not racist, but each day I realize that, if I did not have to do what I have to do in my country, maybe I would come here to join you.

I am at your disposal for any kind of question; no secrets or ceremonies or diplomacy with you.

QUESTION: I am from Mali. I don't know how comfortable you will be with this question, but given the nature of the fight you have been leading, are you satisfied with the type of moral, political, and military aid you have been receiving from other African countries?

CABRAL: First of all, let me say to my brother that I am comfortable with any kind of question—there is no problem. Secondly, when one is in a condition that he has to receive aid, he is never satisfied. The condition of people who are obliged by circumstances to ask for and receive aid is to never be satisfied. If you are satisfied, it is finished; you don't need aid.

Thirdly, we have to also consider the situation of the people who are helping us. You know the political and economic circumstances conditioning the attitudes of the African countries. It's true the past decade of the sixties was a great achievement for Africa—the independence of Africa. But we are not of this tree of independence of Africa. We must take our independence with force and our position is to never ask for the aid we need. We let each people give us the aid they can, and we never accept conditions with the aid. If you cannot give us aid like this, okay, we are satisfied. If you can give more, we are more satisfied.

I have said to the African heads of state many times, that the aid from Africa is very useful, but not sufficient. We believe that they could do better, and so do they. Last June in the Rabat summit meetings [of the OAU] they agreed to increase their aid by 50 percent. Why didn't they do this before? We know that they had not only financial and economic difficulties, but political difficulties as well. In some cases, the difficulty was a lack of consciousness about the importance of this problem. But each day they are realizing more, and maybe when they fully realize the importance of this problem, we will all be independent.

QUESTION: I would like to know what forward thrust your country would have in the absence of NATO support that this country gives, and what the arguments are that the U.S. offers for its participation in NATO, which we all know is the conduit that supplies the Portuguese with their arms? This is something we can take immediate political action on.

CABRAL: You see, Portugal is an underdeveloped country—the most backward in Western Europe. It is a country that doesn't even produce toy planes—this is not a joke, it's true. Portugal would never be able to launch three colonial wars in Africa without the help of NATO, the weapons of NATO, the planes of NATO, the bombs of NATO—it would be impossible for them. This is not a matter for discussion. The Americans know it, the British know it, the French know it very well, the West Germans also know it, and the Portuguese also know it very well.

We cannot talk of American participation in NATO, because NATO is the creation of the United States. Once I came here to the U.S. and I was invited to lunch by the representative of the U.S. on the United Nations' Fourth Committee. He was also the deputy chief of the U.S. delegation to the United Nations. I told him we are fighting against Portuguese colonialism, and not asking for the destruction of NATO. We don't think it is necessary to destroy NATO in order to free our country. But why is the U.S. opposing this? He told me that he did not agree with this policy [U.S. support of NATO], but that there is a problem of world security and, in the opinion of his government, it is necessary to give aid to Portugal in exchange for use of the Azores as a military base. Acceptance of Portuguese policy is necessary for America's global strategy, he explained.

I think he was telling me the truth, but only part of the truth because the U.S. also supports Portugal in order to continue the domination of Africa, if not other parts of the world. I must clarify that this man left his position in the U.N. and, during the debate in the U.S. Congress, took a clear position favorable to ours and asked his government many times to stop its aid to Portugal, but the government didn't accept.

What is the justification for this? There is no justification—no justification at all. It is U.S. imperialism. Portugal is an appendage of imperialism, a rotten appendage of imperialism. You know that Portugal is a semi-colony itself. Since 1775 Portugal has been a semi-colony of Britain. This is the only reason that Portugal was able to preserve the colonies during the partition of Africa. How could this poor, miserable country preserve the colonies in the face of the ambitions and jealousies of Germany, France, England, Belgium, and the emerging American imperialism? It was because England adopted a tactic. It said: Portugal is my colony; if it preserves colonies, they are also my colonies—and England defended the interests of Portugal with force. But now it is not the same. Angola is not really a Portuguese colony. Mozambique is not really a Portuguese colony. You can see the statistics. More than 60 percent of the principal exports of Angola are not for Portugal. Approximately the same percentage of the investments in Angola and Mozambique are not Portuguese, and each day this is increasing. Guinea and Cape Verde are very poor and do not have very good climates. They are the only Portuguese colonies. Portugal is, principally for Angola and Mozambique, the policeman and the receiver of taxes. But they will not tell you this.

QUESTION: My question concerns the basis of law you are using in your country. Are you using the laws of the Portuguese in terms of the National Assembly? What kinds of criteria are you going to use?

CABRAL: If Portugal had created in my country an Assembly, we would not create one ourselves. We don't accept any institution of the Portuguese colonialists. We are not interested in the preservation of any of the structures of the colonial state. It is our opinion that it is necessary to totally destroy, to break, to reduce to ash all aspects of the colonial state in our country in order to make everything possible for our people. The masses realize that this is true, in order to convince everyone we are really finished with colonial domination in our country.

Some independent African states preserved the structures of the colonial state. In some countries they only replaced a White man with a Black man, but for the people it is the same. You have to realize that it is very difficult for the people to make a distinction between one Portuguese, or White, administrator and one Black administrator. For the people, it is the administrator who is fundamental. And the principle—if this administrator, a Black one, is living in the same house, with the same gestures, with the same car, or sometimes a better one, what is the difference? The nature of the state we have to create in our country is a very good question, for it is a fundamental one.

Our fortune is that we are creating the state through the struggle. We now have popular tribunals—people's courts—in our country. We cannot create a judicial system like the Portuguese in our country because it was a colonial one, nor can we even make a copy of the judicial system in Portugal—it is impossible. Through the struggle, we created our courts, and the peasants participate by electing the courts themselves. Ours is a new judicial system, totally different from any other system, born in our country through the struggle. It is similar to other systems, like the one in Vietnam, but it is also different because it corresponds to the conditions of our country.

If you really want to know the feelings of our people on this matter, I can tell you that our government and all its institutions have to take another course. For example, we must not use the houses occupied by the colonial power in the way they used them. I proposed to our party that the government palace in Bissau be transformed into a people's house for culture, not for our prime minister or something like this (I don't believe we will have prime ministers, anyway). This is to let the people realize that they conquered colonialism—it's finished this time—it's not only a question of a change of skin. *This is really very important. It is the most important problem in the liberation movement. The problem of the nature of the state created after independence is perhaps the secret of the failure of African independence.*

QUESTION: Looking at Africa geographically, where does the

PAIGC get most of its support, North Africa, or Sub-Saharan Africa, and in a broader sense, how does support from China and Russia compare?

CABRAL: We don't like this division of Africa. We have the support of the OAU for some years now. We have the total support of the OAU. All the African countries support the PAIGC, no exceptions of any voice against us. And, through the OAU, the Liberation Committee gives us financial help. There are some African countries, maybe not more than the fingers on my hand, that help us directly, also. With them we have bilateral relations. Some are in the north, others in the west, and others in the east.

About China and the Soviet Union, we always had the support of the socialist countries—moral, political, and material. Some have given more material support than others. Until now, the country that has helped us the most is the Soviet Union and, we said it many times before at all kinds of meetings. Until now, they've helped us the most in supplying materials for the war. If you want to verify this, you can come to my country and see. This is the situation.

QUESTION: My question is about the role of women. What is the nature of their transformation from the old system under imperialism?

CABRAL: In our country you find many societies with different traditions and rules on the role of women. For example, in the Fula society, a woman is like a piece of property of the man, the owner of the home. This is the typical patriarchal society. But even there, women have dignity, and if you enter the house, you would see that, inside the house, the woman is the chief. On the other hand, in the Balante society women have more freedom.

To understand these differences, you have to know that, in the Fula society, all that is produced belongs to the father. In the Balante society all that is produced belongs to the people who work, and women work very hard, so they are free. It is very simple. But the problem is about the political role in the fight.

You know that, in our country, there were even matriarchal societies where women were the most important element. On the Bijagos Islands they had queens. They were not queens because they were the daughters of kings. They had queens succeeding queens. The religious leaders were women too. Now they are changing.

I tell you these things so that you can understand our society better. But during the fight, the important thing is the political role of women. Yes, we have made great achievements, but not enough. We are very far from what we want to do, but this is not a problem that can be solved by Cabral signing a decree. It is all a part of the process of transformation, of change in the material conditions of the existence of our people, but also in the minds of the women, because sometimes the greatest difficulty is not only in the men but in the women too.

We have a big problem with our nurses, because we trained about three hundred nurses—women—but they married, they get children, and for them it's finished. This is very bad. For some, this doesn't happen. Carmen Pereira, for instance, is a nurse, and she is also a member of the high political staff of the Party. She is responsible for all social and cultural problems in the southern liberated region. She's a member of the Executive Committee of the Party. There are many others, too, trained not only in the country but in the exterior also, in foreign countries. But we have much work to do.

In the beginning of the struggle, when we launched the guerrilla struggle, young women came without being called and asked for weapons to fight, hundreds and hundreds. But, step by step, some problems came in this framework and we had to distribute, to partition the war. Today, women are principally in what you call the local armed forces and in the political war—working on health problems, and instruction also.

I hope we can send some of our women here so you will be able to know them. But we have big problems to solve and we have a great problem with some of the leaders of the Party. We have (even myself) to combat ourselves on this problem, because we have to be able to cut this cultural element, with its deep roots, until the day we put down this bad thing—the exploitation of women. But we made great progress in this field in these ten years.

QUESTION: Comrade Cabral, you spoke about universal scientific laws of revolution. It is very clear that, in this country, we, too, are engaged in some stage of development of a revolutionary struggle. Certainly, one of the most controversial aspects of our struggle is the grasp of these scientific universal laws. Would you, therefore, talk about your Party's understanding of revolutionary theory, particularly as related to Cuba, China, the Soviet Union, and the anticolonial wars of national liberation? It is very clear that, on the international level, there are defined positions being taken that are probably more important in countries and parties that have defined positions than they are in our struggle, which is so fractured that we play little part in this international struggle for the clarification of these universal scientific laws. So I wonder, would you speak on this problem?

CABRAL: You see, I think that all kinds of struggle for liberation obey a group of laws. The application of these laws to a certain case depends on the nature of the case. Maybe all these laws are applicable, but maybe only some, maybe only one, it depends. In science you know water boils at 100°C. It's a law. Naturally, with the condition that we are speaking in centigrade degrees, this is a specification. What does it mean if we are measuring Fahrenheit? It's not the same. And this is also only at sea level. When you go up in the mountains, this law is not true. Newton and many others told us it is the same, but Einstein demonstrated that it is not always true. It is sometimes more complex.

It's the same in the field of the scientific character of the liberation struggle. Cuba, Soviet Union, China, Vietnam, and so on—our country—are different entities in this context. Sometimes you cannot even explain conflicts between their people because of the different nature of their struggle, dictated by the different conditions of the countries—historical, economical, and so on.

I have to tell you that when we began preparing for our struggle in our own country, we didn't know Mao Tse-tung. The first time I faced a book of Mao Tse-tung was in 1960. Our party was created in 1956. We knew less about the struggle of Cuba, but later we tried to know the experiences of other peoples. Some experiences we put aside because the difference was so great that it would waste time to study them. We think the experiences of other people are very important for you, principally to know the things you should not do. Because what you have to do in your country, you have to create yourself.

The general laws are very simple. For instance, the development of the armed fight in a country characterized by agriculture, where most, if not all, of the population are peasants, means you have to do the struggle as in China, in Vietnam, or in my country. Maybe you begin in the towns, but you recognize that this is not good. You pass to the countryside to mobilize the peasants. You recognize that the peasants are very difficult to mobilize under certain conditions, but you launch the armed struggle and, step by step, you approach the towns in order to finish the colonists.

For instance, this is scientific: in the colonial war there is a contradiction. What is it? It is that the colonial power, in order to really dominate the country, has to disperse its forces. In dispersing its forces, it becomes weak—the national forces can destroy them. As you begin to destroy them, they are obliged to concentrate, but when they concentrate, they leave areas of the country you can control, administer, and create structures in. Then they can never destroy you. It's always possible. You can tell me it's not possible in the United States, the United States is not an agricultural country like this. But if you study deeply the conditions in your country, maybe you will find that this law is also applicable. This is what I can tell you, because it is a very big problem to discuss, if I understood your question.

QUESTION (cont'd): I'd like to rephrase part of it. What I'm trying to get at is how, in setting up the cadre training school that you set up in Conakry, did you have access to the revolutionary experiences of the countries I mentioned? What kind of literature did you read? The point that I am trying to drive at is not the form of waging a revolutionary struggle. I understand the differences in concrete conditions. I want to know how one moves through a colonial or a semifeudal condition into socialism—how the experience of moving from capitalism into socialism (clearly the dominant revolutionary experience in the world) was gained—how you were able to set up a training program in which cadres were exposed to this information?

CABRAL: In the beginning we established in Conakry what you call a political school for militants. About one thousand people came from our country by groups. We first asked, Who are we? Where are we? What do we want? How do we live? What is our enemy? Who is this enemy? What can he do against us? What is our country? Where is our country? Things like this, step by step, explaining our real conditions and explaining what we want, why we want it, and why we have to fight against the Portuguese. Among all these people, some step by step, approached other experiences. But the problem of going from feudal or semifeudal society or tribal society to socialism is a very big problem, even from capitalism to socialism.

If there are Marxists here, they know that Marx said that capitalism created all the conditions for socialism. The conditions were created but never passed. Even then it was very difficult. This is even more reason for the feudal or semifeudal tribal societies to jump to socialism—but it's not a problem of jumping. It's a process of development. You have to establish the political aims, and based on your own condition, the ideological content of the fight. To have ideology doesn't necessarily mean that you have to define whether you are communist, socialist, or something like this. To have ideology is to know what you want in your own condition.

We want in our country this: To have no more exploitation of our people, not by white people nor by Black people. We don't want any more exploitation. It is in this way we educate our people—the masses, the cadres, the militant. For that, we are taking, step by step, all the measures necessary to avoid this exploitation. How? We give to our people the instrument to control, the people lead. And we give to our people all possibilities to participate more actively each day in the direction of their own life.

Naturally, if an American comes, he may say you are doing socialism in your country. This is a responsibility for him. We are not preoccupied with labels, you see. We are occupied in the content of the thing, what we are doing, how we are doing it, what chances are we creating for realizing this aim. There are some societies that passed from feudal or semifeudal stages to being socialist societies. But one of their specifics was having a state imposing this passage. We do not have this. We have to create for ourselves the instruments of the state inside our country, in the conditions of our history, in order to orientate all to a life of justice, work for progress, and equality. Equality of chance for all people is the problem. The problem of equality is equality of chance. This is what I can tell you. This is a very big discussion, philosophical if you want something like this.

QUESTION: What direct relationship does the OAU have with your party? You mentioned the OAU several times, and I heard some things about the OAU, but I wanted to know whether or not it has been helpful to you and, if it has, in what ways?

CABRAL: Yes, they are good relations. Now we can even tell that we are nearly members of the OAU, because, at the last summit conference in Rabat, they admitted the recognized liberation movements, like my party, to participate in the debate concerning their own cases. The relations are very good. We have the help of the OAU, like I said—not enough, we think, but they are trying to increase this help, and we think that, in our own case, maybe next year, we will be a member, full member of the OAU.

QUESTION (cont'd): Why? Do you see it as the organization for Africa?
CABRAL: A real organization for Africa? It depends. Now, at this stage of the revolution in Africa, the OAU is a very good thing. It is such a good thing that imperialism is doing its best to finish it. Naturally, maybe for your ideas, the OAU doesn't answer well, doesn't fully correspond to your hopes. Maybe you are right, but this is not the problem. In the political field, you have to know at each stage if you are doing the possible or not, and preparing the field for the possible for tomorrow or not. This is the problem.

QUESTION (cont'd): Yes, but how was it created and how is it being supported?
CABRAL: Oh, that's a very big matter. You don't know how it was created? They met in May in 1963 in Addis Ababa, and they established a charter.

QUESTION (cont'd): Who is supporting this organization?
CABRAL: Who is supporting it? The states—the African states? Yes the African states. The imperialists—no, you are not right. You are not right, my sister, We can tell that some of the African states . . . (interrupted)

QUESTION (cont'd): If there is such an organization, why are we still where we are? It is just the leaders that elect to go there, not the kind of people like yourself, who are coming down to the masses and speaking the truth. These are neocolonial leaders.
CABRAL: No. But that is not the problem. You are confused. You are making a mistake. One problem is the problem of OAU. The OAU is an organization of African states, it's true. The African states pay to the OAU their respective dues, it's true. Are imperialists supporting the OAU? On the contrary, they do their best not to, because there is a potential danger for them. The other problem is: Are these African states all really independent? Some of them are neocolonialist, but you have to

distinguish this thing in order to do something. If you confuse all—it's not possible.

QUESTION (cont'd): But brother, why is it that each time the question of Pan-Africanism is brought to the discussion, most of them take different views?

CABRAL: Oh yes. You see, you cannot demand all the African states to agree immediately on Pan-Africanism. Even if we discuss Pan-Africanism, you would be surprised. I am for Pan-Africanism. I am for African unity. But we have to be for these things and do them, when possible, not to do it now. You see, my sister, you here in the United States, we understand you. You are for Pan-Africanism and you want it today. Pan-Africanism now! We are in Africa; don't confuse this reaction against Pan-Africanism with the situation of the OAU. I can tell you, the head of state in Africa I admired the most in my life was Nkrumah.

QUESTION (cont'd): He was the only one. He was the father.

CABRAL: Nkrumah was not the father of Pan-Africanism. An American, Du Bois, was the father, if you want. Pan-Africanism is a means to return to the source. You see, it's a very big problem. It's not like this. You are looking at the surface. It's not like this. Nkrumah told me in Conakry—unfortunately he is not alive, but I am not lying, I never lied in my life—he was one of my best friends, I'll never forget him; and you can read my speech at his memorial. You see, he told me, "Cabral, I tell you one thing, our problem of African unity is very important, really, but now if I had to begin again, my approach would be different."

Unfortunately, I am leaving, but if not, I would like very much to speak with you in order to show you Pan-Africanism is a very nice idea; but we have to work for it, and it is not for me to accuse Houphouet-Boigny or Mobutu, because they don't want it. They cannot want it! It is more difficult for some heads of state in Africa to accept African unity as defined by Nkrumah than it is for them to come here to the most racist of the white racists and tell them to accept equal rights for all Africa. You see, more difficult. It's a great problem, my sister. And we think on this problem every day because our future concerns that.

We have a meeting at half past seven with the Chairman of the Decolonization Committee. We have to go there. It is about twenty minutes from here. I am late.

QUESTION: When will we see you again?
CABRAL: Again? I never know. It is difficult for me, but I hope in two years. Also for some of you, if you want, you can come to my country and see me and see our people.

QUESTION: How?
CABRAL: By paying the travel. [*Laughter*]

QUESTION: What are some of the specific financial and political things we can do to further the struggle?
CABRAL: Personally, I don't agree with that question. I think that this meeting is a meeting of brothers and sisters. You represent several organizations. I am very glad because we want your unity. We know it's very difficult—it's more difficult to make your unity than Pan-Africanism, maybe. But we would like you to consider this meeting a meeting between brothers and sisters trying to reinforce, not only our links in blood and in history, but also in aims. I am very glad to have been here with you and I deeply regret that it is not possible to be with you longer. Thank you very much.

— 8 —

New Year's Message

This is the New Year's Message of January, 1973, delivered by Cabral to the PAIGC. It was the last written statement by Cabral to the people of Guinea and the Cape Verde Islands. In that respect, it is the political testament of Amilcar Cabral. In this document, he analyzes what progress has been made and the nature of the struggle yet to come.

Comrades, Compatriots: At this time, as we commemorate a new year of life and struggle, and a year in which our people's fight for independence is ten years old, I must remind everyone—militants, fighters, leaders, and responsible people in our Party—that it is time for action and not words. Action that must daily become more vigorous and effective in Guinea in order to inflict greater defeats on the Portuguese colonialists, and to remove all their vain and criminal pretensions of reconquering our country. Action, too, that must develop daily and become more organized in the Cape Verde Islands, so as to lead the struggle into a new phase, in harmony with the aspirations of our people and the requirements of the total liberation of our country.

I wish, however, to respect tradition by addressing a few words to you at a time when all sane people—those who want peace, liberty, and happiness for all men—renew their hopes and belief in a better life for humanity, belief in dignity and in the independence and progress of all peoples.

As everyone knows, in the past year we have achieved general elections in the liberated areas, with universal suffrage and a secret vote, for the creation of Regional Councils and the first National Assembly in the history of our people. In all sectors of all the regions, the elections were conducted in an atmosphere of great enthusiasm among the population. The electorate voted massively from the lists that had been prepared throughout eight months of public and democratic debates, in the course of which the representatives for each sector were selected. Once assembled, the elected Regional Councils elected, in their turn, representatives to the National Popular Assembly from among their members. This will have 120 members, of which 80 will have been drawn from the popular masses and 40 from the political cadres, the military, the technicians and others of the Party. As you know, the representatives of the sectors temporarily occupied by the colonialists have been chosen provisionally.

And so, today, our African Peoples of Guinea possess a new means of sovereignty: their National Assembly. This will be in accordance with the Constitution we are preparing, the supreme medium of the sovereignty of our people in Guinea. Tomorrow, with the certain advance of the struggle, we will create in the same way the first National Popular Assembly of the Cape Verde Islands. The combined meeting of the members of these two organs will constitute the Supreme Assembly of the People of Guinea and the Cape Verde Islands.

The creation of the first National Popular Assembly in Guinea is a victory that transcends even the difficult but glorious struggle of our people for independence. It opens new perspectives for the progress of our politico-military action; it is the result of the effort and willing sacrifice of our people through ten years of armed struggle; it is a concrete proof of the sovereignty of our people and of their high level of patriotic and national consciousness. I wish, therefore, at this time, to warmly congratulate our people and all of the electorate who, as conscious men and women, have been able to accomplish their duty as free citizens of our African nation with such dignity. I wish to congratulate also all the militants, organizers, and leaders who, in electoral committees or in other kinds of activities, have contributed to the success of this venture, the achievement of which will live in the history of our country. I congratulate the brave fighters of our armed forces with equal enthusiasm. By their courageous action they have created in all sectors the security needed for holding the elections, despite the criminal attempts of the colonialist enemy to stop them taking place.

A National Assembly, however, like any organ in any living body, must be able to function in order to justify its existence. We thus have a major task ahead of us, to be accomplished within the framework of our struggle in this new year of 1973: We must make our National Popular Assembly work. And this we shall do, thereby implementing the decisions taken by our great Party at the meeting of the Supreme Council of the Struggle, held in August 1971, decisions that are upheld by the people with great enthusiasm.

In the course of this coming year and as soon as it is conveniently possible, we shall call a meeting of the National Popular Assembly in Guinea in order to accomplish the first historic mission incumbent upon it: the proclamation of our State, the creation of an Executive for this State, and the promulgation of a fundamental Law—the first Constitution in our history—which will be the basis of the active life of our African nation. That is to say, legitimate representatives of our people, chosen by the people and freely elected by patriotic and responsible citizens of our country, will proceed with the most important act of their lives and in the lives of our people: that of stating to the world that our African Nation, forged in the struggle, has irreversibly decided to move towards independence without waiting for the consent of the Portuguese colonialists, and that, dating from this statement, the Executive of our State will be, under the direction of our Party, the PAIGC, the only true and legitimate representative of our people in everything, national and international, that concerns it.

We are moving from the position of a colony that has a Liberation Movement and that the people have already liberated, in ten years of armed struggle, the greater part of its national territory, to the position of a country that runs its own State and that has a part of its national territory occupied by foreign armed forces.

This radical change in the situation in our country corresponds to the concrete reality of the life and struggle of our people in Guinea; it is based on the concrete results of our struggle and has the firm support of all African peoples and governments, as well as that of the anti-colonialist and anti-racist forces of the world. It also adheres to the principles of the United Nations Charter and to the resolutions adopted by this international organization, notably in its 27th Session.

Nothing, no criminal action or illusionist maneuver by the Portuguese colonialists, can stop our African people, masters of their own destinies and aware of their rights and duties, from taking this decisive and transcendent step towards the achievement of the fundamental objective of our struggle: the conquest of national independence and the building, in restored peace and dignity, of its true advancement under the exclusive direction of its own children, beneath the glorious flag of our Party.

The particular importance of the formation of the National Popular Assembly, of the proclamation of the State of Guinea, and of the creation of its corresponding executive membership, who will be neither provisional—neither will they live in exile—necessarily implies much greater responsibilities for our people, and in particular for the militants, the fighters, the organizers, and the leaders of our Party. These historic undertakings demand greater effort and daily sacrifice on our part, further thought to ensure better action, further activity to ensure better thought. We must think about each specific problem that we have to resolve in such a way as to find the best solution for it under the particular conditions of our country and our struggle. These undertakings also require that we intensify and further develop our political and military action in Guinea without, however, neglecting the important activities that we are carrying out in the economic, social, and cultural fields. They demand that we successfully deploy the necessary effort for the advance of the political struggle in the Cape Verde Islands and in order that our people should, as soon as possible, move into systematic direct action against the Portuguese colonialists.

Under these conditions, we cannot for one moment forget that we are at war and that the main enemy of our people and of Africa—the fascist Portuguese colonialists—still nourish, with the blood and misery of their people and by underhanded maneuvers and savage acts, the criminal intention and vain hope of destroying our Party, of annihilating our struggle, and recolonizing our people. Our attention and the best of our energy and effort must be devoted to the armed struggle, to war, to concrete action by both our local and our national armed forces. We must also, in 1973, set in motion all our human and material capability and ability in order to inject even greater intensity into the struggle on all fronts and extract the greatest profit from men, arms, and the experience we have, thereby to inflict even greater blows on the colonialist enemy by destroying an even larger number of their living forces. For the history of colonial warfare, as well as our own experience over ten years of struggle, have taught us that the colonial aggressors—and the Portuguese colonial aggressors in particular—only understand the language of force and only measure reality by the number of corpses.

It is true that in 1972 we inflicted great defeats and important losses on the Portuguese aggressors. In a few days, our Information Service will publish the account of our actions over the past year, which will be widely reported by our broadcasting station "Radio Libertacao," as well as by other means of information. But we must recognize that the enemy, possessing more planes and helicopters provided by its allies in NATO, has significantly increased its bombing and terrorist raids against our liberated regions; it has attempted and still tries to create difficult conditions for us with its plots for the reoccupation of a certain number of localities in these regions. Above all, we must recognize that, with the manpower, arms, and experience that we possess, we could and should have done more and better. This is what we must do and certainly will do in 1973, especially as we are going to use more powerful arms and other instruments of war on all fronts.

Basing ourselves on a greater number of better trained cadres and fighters, strengthened by greater experience, we are going to make more efficient use of all the means presently at our disposal, and of those that we will have in the future, inflicting decisive and mortal blows on the criminal colonialists.

Parallel to our intensification of armed action on all fronts, we must be capable of developing our action behind and at the heart of the enemy, and where it feels itself to be most secure. I wish to congratulate the courageous militants who, by their decisive action, have inflicted some important blows against the enemy over the past year, particularly in Bissau, Bafata, and Bula. But I also draw everyone's attention to the need to develop and intensify this kind of action.

In fact, the time has come when, based on solid and efficient clandestine organization, there should be the destruction of the greatest possible number of the human and material assets of the Portuguese colonialists in the urban centers of our country. In fact, we are facing a savage enemy that does not have the slightest scruple in its criminal activities, that has access to every possible means of attempting to destroy us wherever we are. Also, since we are fighting in our country for the sacred right of our people to independence, peace, and true progress, we must at this decisive moment attack the colonialist and racist enemy—itself, its agents, its assets—with destructive blows, wherever they are. This is an urgent task to which all organizers and militants of this part of the struggle must dedicate themselves with the greatest attention; particularly those comrades who, with courage and decisiveness, are active in the centers and areas still occupied by the enemy.

I would like to mention here an important problem that we are facing in the colonial war—the huge attempts by the enemy to occupy or reoccupy a certain number of the localities of the liberated areas. I wish to remind the comrades of the Party and our people that these attempts, such as bombing and terrorist assaults, successful or not, are characteristic of colonial warfare. They are necessarily part of the action of the colonialist aggressor, especially when the patriotic forces have liberated the greater part of the national territory, as in our case. We must therefore face this problem realistically and give it its proper evaluation within the general context of our struggle, without either exaggerating or diminishing its importance.

As the comrades and especially the leaders and organizers of the Party know, in the context of its colonial war, the colonial aggressor is coming up against a fundamental contradiction, that has no solution and with which it struggles throughout the war. It is the following: so as to feel that it dominates the territory, it is forced to disperse its troops to enable them to occupy the greatest possible number of positions. This makes it weaker, and the concentrated patriotic forces are able to direct hard and mortal blows at it. This forces it to retreat, to enable it to concentrate its troops and try to avoid losing a great many human lives and be able to resist the advancing nationalist forces and gain time against them. But, by concentrating its troops, its military and political presence ceases to exist over vast areas of the country, which are organized and administered by the patriotic forces.

Blinded by the despair brought on by defeats to which it has been subjected and is still subjected both in our country and internationally, in the present phase of our struggle and of the Portuguese colonial war, the enemy tries vainly to make the

Corubal River return to Fouta Djalou instead of flowing towards the Goba and the sea. This attempt, like that of tricking our people with the mirage of the "Better Guinea," à la Portugal, and that of making African fight African, is doomed to failure. The enemy will never free itself from the basic contradiction of its dirty colonial war.

What is important for us, with our knowledge of the strategy that the enemy is forced to use by the objective laws of colonial warfare, is not to worry too much when the enemy tries to settle in Gompara, Cabochanque, Cadique, or in other places. What is important is, on the one hand, to carry forward our own battle plans and, on the other, to do our best to destroy the greatest number of living enemy forces whenever they settle or move to take up a position in any part of our liberated areas. What counts is to aim heavy blows at them, to allow them no rest, to turn any occupied position into a graveyard for their troops, until they are forced to retreat, as we have done in Blana, Gadembel, and more recently in Tabanca Nova in the Cubiseco Region. This we must do, and will certainly do, to any position that the enemy occupies inside the liberated areas. It is what we must also do to the barracks and entrenched camps still in our country.

Naturally, in 1973 we must continue to intensify our political work among the popular masses, both inside the liberated areas and the occupied zones of Guinea, and on the Cape Verde Islands. Without wishing to diminish the value of the work already done in this field, which produced the failure of the so-called "Better Guinea" policy—a policy as false as the boasts that were made about it—we must recognize that there are some sectors where political action is still deficient. In this coming year we must make every effort to improve our activities in these areas for, as we know, however important our armed action is, our struggle is a thoroughly political one that aims at a specific political objective: the independence and progress of our country.

While I congratulate the comrades who, both in Guinea and on the Cape Verde Islands, have bettered their political work throughout the past year, I encourage everyone to double their efforts in consolidating and developing the political conquests of the Party and the struggle, so that each day the political consciousness and patriotism of the masses, the militants, and the fighters will be raised higher, strengthening the indestructible unity of our people, the vital basis of the success of our struggle. In this way, in the area of security and control, vigilance will be strengthened towards the enemy and their agents, against all those who, because of opportunism, ambition, and moral weakness or servility towards the enemy, might try to destroy our Party and consequently the just struggle of our people for independence.

On the Cape Verde Islands, the events of September 1972, that formed the first clash between the population of the Archipelago and the forces of colonial oppression, have once again shown the level of tension produced by the political situation. In congratulating the patriots of Praia and Santiago, who acted with courage and decisiveness in the face of provocation by the colonialists and their agents, I wish to encourage them continually to improve their clandestine organization, to act with sureness and without allowing the enemy to destroy the nationalist cadres, and to prepare themselves by every means within their reach for the new phase of our struggle in the Archipelago, which is forced ahead by the criminal stubbornness of the Portuguese colonialists. I wish to stress that the Party executive is more determined than ever to put everything into developing the struggle on the Cape Verde Islands.

Looking back on the progress already made and at the complexity of the specific problems to be solved, it has become necessary and urgent, in my opinion, to proceed with a realistic modification inside the structure of the Party to enable a certain number of comrades to devote themselves entirely to the development of the struggle on the Cape Verde Islands. Such a modification will be proposed at the next meeting of the Party executive.

Still, on the political front, I draw the attention of the comrades to the diversity of the new problems that we have to study in an efficient manner, problems arising from the new perspectives of the development of the struggle that will be opened up by the proclamation of the state of Guinea: in the interior, improvement and development of the administrative services, creation of controlling bodies for our activities, a new census of the population with identification of all its component elements, etc.; and in the exterior, organization, control, and protection of emigrant citizens, their identification, and a corresponding distribution of passports, mobilization for the struggle, etc., without going into the kinds of relations to be established on the international front. These are certainly new problems, and very important ones, that we must study deeply and resolve in time.

The preoccupation of war and political work must not, however, make us forget or underestimate the importance of our activities on the economic, social, and cultural front that are the foundations of the new life we are creating inside the liberated regions. We must all, especially the cadres that specialize in these matters, pay our best attention to the problems of the economy, health, social welfare, education, and culture, to improve our work significantly and be able to resolve the vast problems we have to face in this new phase of our struggle. With this in view, we must now steadfastly and determinedly face up to our major concerns: the feeding of the people, the improvement of living conditions for the population, taxes, the exchequer, the new financial life that we hope to establish, the money we will use, etc., as well as the kind of social security to be evolved based on our experience, school curricula, and the forming of new centers for national reconstruction and the building of our people's progress. So many new problems, complex certainly, but invigorating, that we must resolve while we continue to intensify and develop vigorous politico-military action to expel the colonialist troops from the positions they still occupy in Guinea and the Cape Verde Islands. The specialist groups in the Party will have to devote their attention to the study and solution of these problems, in order to accomplish their duty towards the people.

In the name of the Party executive, I congratulate the agricultural workers of Guinea for the crops they harvested last year, despite the scarcity of rain. I wish to encourage them to do more and better this year to ensure a good crop for, as we know, therein lies the main base of our life and struggle, and the Portuguese try to destroy it by every means in their power when they find themselves unable to steal the fruits of our people's labors.

But it is with sadness that I now remember that at this moment the population of the Cape Verde Islands is menaced by famine. This is the Portuguese colonialists' fault because they have never wished nor thought to create the economic and social conditions in the Archipelago to ensure the subsistence, at a decent level, of the population in very dry years. Forced by the advance of the struggle and by the denunciations of the Party to the world, the fascist colonial government of Portugal granted loans and subsidies to the Cape Verde Islands to, as the colonialists say, "attenuate the crisis." That is to say, in order to prevent too many people dying of starvation at one time, although without stopping the weak, especially children, from dying of specific hunger or even total starvation. I raise my voice once again in the name of the Party executive to protest against this situation and to denounce the crime perpetrated by the fascist colonial government of Lisbon in transporting to Portugal fifteen or twenty thousand young Cape Verdeans to work in the mines, sweep the streets in the main cities, and do unskilled labor. This is done with the ulterior aim of barring the way to progress in our liberation struggle, causing a great loss of vital strength from the Cape Verde Islands. I appeal to all Cape Verdean and Guinean patriots living in Portugal to keep in close contact and organize themselves towards uniting with all the forced laborers transferred from the Cape Verde Islands, developing their patriotic activities in the service of the Party, our people, and Africa. Thus, at the right moment, they should be able to aim hard blows at the enemy with the result that the takers are in turn taken.

I draw the attention of those responsible for the revictualling of the population, especially those who work in the people's shops, to the fact that, this year, the Party will possess greater quantities than ever before of urgently needed articles. We must be able to place them at the disposal of the population of all the liberated areas, whatever the difficulties we may face in so doing. In fact, we have received aid from socialist countries, in particular the Soviet Union, Sweden, Norway, and other countries, as well as from humanitarian organizations. This aid will afford us great improvements in the functioning of the people's shops, as well as of health and educational institutions.

I hope that everyone will make the necessary effort to ensure that 1973 will be a period of greater efficiency still in the revictualling of our population in articles of primary necessity.

As everyone knows, 1972 was a year of great and decisive international victories by our great Party and our people. Among the main achievements I wish to remind you of the following:

- The now historic visit of the United Nations Special Mission to the liberated areas of our country, which brought great results for the prestige, not only of our Party and the struggle, but also to all the African Liberation Movements. While recalling this event, which the Portuguese colonial aggressors wished to oppose with their most violent crimes, I salute in this new year the peoples of Ecuador, Sweden, Tunisia, Senegal, and Japan, whose courageous children visited our country as members of the special mission. I thank their respective governments for having allowed their representatives to make such a visit, and the Secretary General of the United Nations for the firm way in which he applied a great historic resolution of the General Assembly of that international organization.
- The Resolution of the Decolonization Committee of the United Nations in its session in April 1972, by which our Party was recognized by general acclamation as being the only true and legitimate representative of the peoples of Guinea and the Cape Verde Islands.

- The Resolution of the 27th Session of the General Assembly of the United Nations, which, among other vital decisions, confirmed the recognition of our Party as the sole legitimate representative of our African people and requested all the states, governments, and national and international organizations, as well as the specialized agencies of the United Nations, to reinforce their aid to our Party and to always and only deal with it in every circumstance concerning the peoples of Guinea and the Cape Verde Islands.
- The historic resolution of the Security Council, which, under its first woman President, our Guinean sister and comrade Jeanne Martin Cisse, unanimously adopted a resolution condemning Portuguese colonialism and demanding the Portuguese government stop the colonial war in Africa, withdraw its occupying troops, and enter into negotiations with the respective patriotic forces that, in our country, are represented by our Party. For the first time in the diplomatic and political struggle against Portuguese colonialism, our Party spoke at the United Nations with the status of Observer; even the allies of the fascist colonial government of Portugal voted in unison against it in the United Nations Security Council. This resolution has, and will have, great significance in the future development of our politico-military actions to expel the criminal Portuguese colonial aggressors.
- Finally, but not least, I remember the resolutions of solidarity and unconditional total support adopted by the conference of the African heads of state and governments in Rabat, at which our Party was once again chosen as spokesman for all the African Liberation Movements.

This past year has been full of great international victories, made more so by the fact that we are sure of the moral, political, and, in some cases, material support of the independent African states. Firstly, the neighboring and fraternal countries, the Republics of Guinea and Senegal, as well as that of all the anti-colonialist and anti-racist countries and forces. We have received, or are about to receive in this coming year, further material from the Soviet Union and from all the other socialist countries; from Sweden, Norway, Denmark, Finland; various parties and political organizations in Europe; and from humanitarian institutions like the World Council of Churches, Rowntree in England, the World Church Service of America, the French Popular Aid, the International Red Cross, and various other support committees established around the world. Specialized or autonomous departments of the United Nations, like the African Economic Committee, UNESCO, UNICEF, WHO, the High Commission for Refugees, and the ILO [International Labor Organization] are and will continue to increase their cooperation with our Party, and tomorrow, surely, with our State.

Comrades and Compatriots, you now understand why the fascist colonial government of Marcelo Caetano and its representatives in our country find reason to despair. You will also understand why, given their unscrupulous and contemptuous attitudes towards the rights of all peoples, including their own, they resort to any means and crimes with which to try and stop our struggle. You understand now why the Portuguese colonial aggressors and their leader in our country are more vicious than ever, and intensify their bombing, multiply their assaults on our liberated areas, and make every effort to try and reoccupy a certain number of places inside these areas. It is in order to console themselves for the military, political, and diplomatic defeats that we inflict upon them; it is in order to try, with every new crime they perpetrate, to demoralize our forces and demobilize our population. It is the defeats they endured in 1972 in our country, in Africa and abroad that explain the heightened aggression against our liberated areas, especially in Cubacare, which was visited in April by the United Nations Special Mission.

The despair of the fascist Portuguese colonial government is even more understandable, now that it is certain that the "better Guinea policy" has totally failed, and it is certain that the lie about a "better Cape Verde" policy will also fail. As far as Guinea is concerned, it is the fascist colonial government in Lisbon itself which, with the voice of the head of the criminal colonial aggressors, confesses to this defeat while stating at the same time that what the African wants is to have "his own political and social voice." It is exactly what the Africans of Guinea and Cape Verde Islands want. But we call that independence, that is to say, the total sovereignty of our people nationally and internationally, to build himself, in peace and dignity through his own efforts and sacrifices, walking on his own two feet and guided by his own head, the progress that is his right, like all the peoples of the world. And this must come about in cooperation with other peoples, including the people of Portugal who, in the course of three liberation wars against Castile or Spain, fought to conquer *their own social and political voice*, their own independence—and won.

Also, as you know, while the populations of the colonialist occupied urban centers show an increasing interest in the Party and the struggles, proved by the great number of young people who have abandoned Bissau and other towns to join the combat, the situation in Portugal is deteriorating with gathering speed, and the Portuguese people are voicing their opposition to the colonial war with increasing clamor. The fascist colonial government in Lisbon and its agents in our country are pressurized into seeking to ascertain whether they can change the situation before their cause becomes completely lost in their own country.

But they are wasting their time and lose the lives of the young Portuguese they send to war ingloriously and in vain. They will continue to perpetrate crimes against our populace; they will make a lot more attempts at destroying our Party and our struggle. Without a doubt, they will take shameless aggressive action against neighboring countries. But all in vain. For no crime, no use of force, no maneuver in word or deed of the criminal Portuguese colonial aggressors will be able to stop the march of history, the irreversible march of our own African people of

Guinea and the Cape Verde Islands towards their independence.

Forward, comrades and compatriots in the historic struggle for National Liberation! Health, long life, and increasing success to our African People, our courageous fighters, to all the militants, organizers and leaders of our great Party!

Let us proclaim the existence of our State in Guinea and advance with the victorious struggle of our people in the Cape Verde Islands!

Long live the PAIGC, strength and guide of our people, in Guinea and the Cape Verde Islands!

Death to the criminal Portuguese colonial aggressors!

Notes

Introduction to the Second Edition

All emphases in the original unless otherwise indicated.

1. *Lumumba Speaks*, the speeches and writings of Patrice Lumumba 1958–1961, edited by Jean Van Lierde, translated from the French by Helen R. Lane, and introduced by Jean-Paul Sartre (Boston, MA: Little, Brown and Co., 1972), 429.
2. For a concise exposition of this period, see Peter Karibe Mendy, *Amílcar Cabral: A Nationalist and Pan-Africanist Revolutionary* (Athens, OH: Ohio University Press, 2019), 55–75.
3. My translation of a portion of an interview, "Amilcar Cabral Guinee Bissau Cap-Vert," YouTube Video, 4:46, September 4, 2009, http://www.youtube.com/watch?v=_O-obP3r6Hw.
4. Aimé Césaire, *Discours sur le Colonialisme* (Dakar, Senegal: Présence Africaine, 1955), 19. *Discourse on Colonialism* (New York: Monthly Review Press, 1972), 21.
5. Frantz Fanon, *Les damnés de la terre* (Paris, France: La Découverte, 2002), 40. *The Wretched of the Earth* (New York: Grove Press, 1968), 36–37.
6. This is, within the African context, what Marx refers to, in the second paragraph of the *Third Thesis on Feuerbach*, when he states: "The coincidence of the changing of circumstance and of human activity or self-changing can be conceived and rationally understood only as *revolutionary practice*." "Thesis on Feuerbach" (1845), in *The German Ideology*, supplementary texts (New York: International Publishers, 1973), 121.
7. Marcien Towa, *L'idée d'une philosophie négro-africaine* (Yaoundé, Cameroun: Editions CLE, 1979), 71.
8. Tsenay Serequeberhan, *The Hermeneutics of African Philosophy: Horizon*

and Discourse (New York: Routledge, 1994), 102–115, and 118, the last paragraph of section one. See also, Louis-Dominique Biakolo Komo, "The Hermeneutical Paradigm in African Philosophy," in *Nokoko*, 2017, no.16, *Journal of the Institute of African Studies*, Carlton University, Ottawa Canada, https://carleton.ca/africanstudies/wp-content/uploads/Nokoko-6-08-The-Hermeneutical-Paradigm-in-African-Philosophy-Genesis-Evolution-and-Issues.pdf.

9. Bill Ashcroft, Gareth Griffiths, and Helen Tiffin, eds., *The Post-Colonial Reader,* second edition (New York: Routledge, 2006), 1–2.
10. On this point, see Tsenay Serequeberhan, *Existence and Heritage* (New York: SUNY Press, 2015), chapter 1 and specifically the remarks to endnote 77, on 138.
11. Antonio Gramsci, *Quaderni Del Carcere*, vol. 2, edizione critica dell'Instituto Gramsci, a cura di Valentino Gerratana (Torino: Giulio Einaudi, 1975), 1376. *Selections from the Prison Notebooks of Antonio Gramsci*, ed. and trans. Q. Hoare and G. N. Smith (New York: International Publishers, 1971), 324.
12. Aimé Césaire, *Lettre à Maurice Thorez* (Paris: Présence Africaine, 1956), 12.
13. Ibid., 8.
14. Ibid., 15–16.
15. Fanon, *Les damnés de la terre*, 197; *The Wretched of the Earth*, 206.

Introduction to the First Edition

1. Declaration made on the release of three Portuguese soldiers taken prisoner by the PAIGC, March 1968.

1. A Question-and-Answer Session, University of London

1. Richard Handyside, Editor, *Revolution in Guinea: Selected Texts* (New York: Monthly Review Press, 1970).

Glossary

Anti-Colonialist Movement (MAC): Started in 1957 in Paris by nationalists from Portuguese colonies studying in Europe, the MAC sought to analyze and unite the African anti-colonial struggle, and became one of the cornerstones of the modern Pan-African movement. The MAC's manifesto was considered by Amilcar Cabral to be essential to the fight against Portuguese colonization. In 1960, the MAC was introduced to the world at the Second Conference of African Peoples, held in Tunis, Tunisia, but soon after dissolved to become part of the African Revolutionary Front for the National Independence of the Portuguese Colonies (FRAIN).

Balante (or Balanta): The largest ethnic group in Guinea-Bissau, comprising around one quarter of the population. The name comes from the Mandinka people of northern Guinea-Bissau, meaning "those who resist."

Dr. Hastings Kamuzu Banda: (1898–1997) Prime minister, then president of the first independent government of Malawi, from 1964 to 1994. His regime was known for its political repression as well as its collaborationist politics with apartheid South Africa and the Portuguese colonies of Africa.

Marcelo Caetano: (1906–1980) Scholar and politician who succeeded António Salazar as Portuguese prime minister. He served from 1968 to 1974, continuing Salazar's corporate dictatorship. With General António de Spínola, Caetano was among the colonialist leaders who targeted Cabral for elimination. International criticism of his policies in African colonies helped to generate the 1974 "Carnation Revolution," which overthrew Portugal's regime and drove Caetano into exile in Brazil.

CLSTP (Committee for the Liberation of São Tomé and Príncipe): Founded in 1960 in São Tomé and Príncipe (one country comprised of two islands) in the Gulf of Guinea, the CLSTP opposed Portuguese colonial rule. Manuel Pinto da Costa, who became president of São Tomé and Príncipe after its independence, was the party's leader. The CLSTP later became the Movement for the Liberation of São Tomé and Príncipe–Social Democratic Party (MLSTP–PSD).

CONCP (Conference of Nationalist Organizations of the Portuguese Colonies): Umbrella organization that coordinated and facilitated communication between various liberation movements and nationalist parties during the People's War in Angola, Mozambique, and Guinea-Bissau (approximately 1961–1974). Formed in 1961 in Casablanca, Morocco, by the PAIGC (Guinea-Bissau, Cape Verde), the MPLA (Angola), FRELIMO (Mozambique), and the CLSTP (São Tomé and Príncipe).

Basil Davidson: (1914–2010) British journalist and historian who wrote more than thirty books about African politics and history, among them, *No Fist Is Big Enough to Hide the Sky: The Liberation of Guinea-Bissau and Cape Verde, 1963–74*.

W. E. B. Du Bois: (1868–1963) Pathbreaking U.S. author, socialist, political thinker, historian, essayist, and civil rights activist, whom Amilcar Cabral called the "father of Pan-Africanism."

ECA (Economic Commission for Africa): United Nations committee, established in 1958 by the UN Economic and Social Council to promote economic cooperation and social development among African countries. The ECA is currently made up of fifty-four member states.

FRELIMO (Front for the Liberation of Mozambique): Originally, a Marxist-Leninist military movement and political party, FRELIMO was formed in 1962 in Tanzania by exiled Mozambicans fighting for Mozambique's liberation from Portugal. After the 1969 assassination of its leader, Eduardo Mondlane, Samora Michel took over as military commander. In 1975, when Mozambique won its independence, FRELIMO became the governing party, and today remains the dominant political party in Mozambique.

Fula (or Fulbe or Fulanis): The second-largest ethnic group of Guinea-Bissau, after the Balante. Historically, the Fula are a pastoral or nomadic people, and today comprise one of the largest ethnic groups in the Sahel and West Africa.

Arthur de Gobineau: (1816–1882) French aristocrat, diplomat, ethnologist, and social thinker who developed a theory of racial determinism that enormously bolstered the development of white supremacism in Europe and the West.

Félix Houphouet-Boigny: (1905?–1993) Politician, physician, and first president of Côte d'Ivoire (Ivory Coast), from that country's independence in 1960 until Houphouet-Boigny's death. Houphouet-Boigny was born into a royal African family and inherited the status of chief, along with a cocoa plantation, at the age of five. During his political career, he sought increasingly to preserve colonial assets by steering clear of communist parties and subverting socialist Pan-African governments, while developing economic liberalism in an effort to cultivate closer ties to France and the West. He was, in his political maneuvering and orientation, in every respect, a neocolonial protégé of France.

Lucian Lévy-Bruhl: (1857–1939) Sorbonne philosophy professor, much of whose work was devoted to the study of the mentality of people in so-called primitive societies. His book, *Les Fonctions mentales dans les sociétés primitives* or *How Natives Think*, written in 1910, became greatly influential among anthropologists.

Mandingues (or Mandika or Mandingo): Descendants of the thirteenth-century Mali empire, these West African people generally speak different dialects of the Mande language and now reside in several West African countries, including Guinea-Bissau. Globally, their population is about eleven million.

Mandjak: A West African people comprising about 14 percent of Guinea-Bissau's population, but also residing in Gambia, Senegal, and Portugal. The Mandjak often refer to themselves as "Manjaku," which, in their Senegalo-Guinean Bak language, means "I tell you."

Mobutu Sese Seko: (1930–1997) Congolese politician, military officer, and president of Democratic Republic of Congo (which he renamed Zaire in 1971) from 1965 to 1997. Although claiming to be politically neither right, left, nor center, he established, early in his regime, a one-man-rule policy, ordering public executions of those he deemed traitors, spies, or rivals. In 1997 rebel forces forced him into exile in Morocco, where he died shortly after.

MPLA (People's Movement for the Liberation of Angola): Formed in 1956, the MPLA joined the PAIGC in 1961 and went on to fight the Portuguese military in the Angolan War of Independence (1961–1974). Since the establishment of Angola's new government in 1975, it has remained Angola's ruling political party.

Kwame Nkrumah: (1909–1972) Ghanaian political theorist and revolutionary who became, after Ghana's independence in 1957, the first president and prime minister, until he was ousted by a CIA-sponsored coup in 1966. Until his death, Nkrumah lived in Guinea, where he was named honorary co-president.

OAU (Organization of African Unity): Founded in 1963 in Addis Ababa, Ethiopia, the OAU was an intergovernmental organization originally involving thirty-two signatory governments. Two of its principal founders were Ethiopian Emperor Haile Selassie and Ghanaian president Kwame Nkrumah. The organization sought to encourage the work of self-determination in African countries and to defend each country's sovereignty and independence. Its summit conference in 1972, in Rabat, Morocco, included representatives of forty African nations, including Amilcar Cabral, the only speaker who was not a head of state. In 2002 the OAU became the African Union (AU), maintaining the OAU's anticolonial founding principles.

PAIGC (African Party for the Independence of Guinea and Cape Verde): Beginning in 1956 as a nonviolent project for nationalist self-determination, the PAIGC was founded by six people, including Amilcar Cabral, who was appointed secretary-general. As Portuguese repression—notably the 1959 massacre of fifty protesting dockworkers—intensified, however, the organization turned to armed struggle. The PAIGC is currently the largest party in Guinea-Bissau's National People's Assembly.

Pan-Africanism: A worldwide movement recognizing the right to self-determination and mutual solidarity of all African peoples, whether living in Africa or the diaspora. Begun spontaneously amid the earliest resistance to the Atlantic slave trade, modern Pan-Africanism took hold in the beginning of the twentieth century, when Henry Sylvester Williams organized the first Pan-African Congress in London, in 1900. Globally, Pan-Africanism's adherents number in the millions and, historically, have included Kwame Nkrumah, Marcus Garvey, Constance Cummings-John, Malcolm X, C. L. R. James, Angela Davis, W. E. B. Du Bois, Patrice Lumumba, Ida B. Wells-Barnett, Amilcar Cabral, and Assata Shakur. The African Union (AU), consisting of fifty-five African member-states, is today considered a base of Pan-Africanism.

António de Oliveira Salazar: (1888–1970) Portuguese prime minister and dictator from 1932 to 1968. In 1933, he helped initiate Portugal's "Estado Novo," a form of corporatized authoritarianism that proved to be one of the most durable fascist regimes in twentieth-century Europe. He was a strong opponent of the self-determination of any Portuguese colony.

António de Spínola: (1990–1996) Military officer, author, and conservative politician who served twice as the Portuguese governor and commander-in-chief of the Armed Forces during the People's War in Angola, Mozambique, and Guinea-Bissau (approximately 1961–1974). Unlike his less genteel peers, he favored a policy of nominal respect for ethnic Guineans. He became president of Portugal after the Carnation Revolution forced Marcelo Caetano from office, and helped to move government power through democratic channels. Four and a half months after taking office, he resigned and fled to Brazil, due largely to the government's shift to the left.

Moïse Tshombe: (1919–1969) Congolese politician, businessman, and president of Katanga, an African state that broke away from Congo-Léopoldville in 1960. Employing covert military help from Belgium and a white mercenary force, Tshombe maintained the Republic of Katanga for three years, despite United Nations and Congolese efforts to end Katanga's secession. He then became prime minister, from 1964 to 1965, of what is now the Democratic Republic of the Congo. His politics were decidedly pro-Western, making him a model African leader for U.S. conservatives.

Index